THE VANIS

C000204691

"Engrossing . . . The boo[k's] ultimate theme is about restoring memory—that most significant feature that makes humans human."

—*THE WASHINGTON POST*

"A heartwarming and fascinating story by a superlatively gifted writer and first-rate reporter. . . . *The Vanished Collection* is a remarkable book."

—*AIR MAIL*

"Riveting . . . This page-turner will delight art history and mystery fans alike."

—*PUBLISHERS WEEKLY*

"Undeniably intriguing . . . memorable and often moving. A fascinating journey to uncover lost family secrets—and treasure."

—*KIRKUS REVIEWS*

"Pauline Baer de Perignon is a natural storyteller—refreshingly honest, curious and open. Like the best memoirists, she manages to tell multiple stories simultaneously, to delicately layer meanings and narratives. Here is not only a riveting art world mystery, but an utterly personal, heartfelt, and extremely intelligent story of a woman doing everything she can to uncover the truths of her family."

—MENACHEM KAISER,
author of *Plunder: A Memoir of Family Property and Nazi Treasure*

"A charmingly told account of a woman's quest to reconstruct her great-grandfather's art collection that leads her not only to the restitution of looted works, but also to a profound and touching recognition of her family's wartime odyssey and her own place in their myriad generations."

—LYNN H. NICHOLAS,
author of *The Rape of Europa: The Fate of Europe's Treasures in the Third Reich and the Second World War*

"Beautifully evokes a vanished world that once stood at the crossroads between the heights of civilization and the depths of barbarism before being overwhelmed by the latter. The restitution to Pauline Baer de Perignon's family of one of France's finest 18th-century masterpieces, through a harrowing process dramatically recounted in this book, goes some way to redeem the cause of civilization."

—JAMES GARDNER,
author of *The Louvre: The Many Lives of the World's Most Famous Museum*

"Stimulated by a desire to write, Pauline unconsciously understands that what she really wants is to bear witness. As if in a Kubrick film, she opens a door and a river of blood pours out on her. With valued assistance from Modiano, Pauline digs into this shocking story that amazes and breaks the heart . . . transforming an unfortunately commonplace account of paintings stolen by the Nazis into a breathtaking novel of suspense."

—*LE FIGARO*

THE
VANISHED
COLLECTION

THE VANISHED COLLECTION

Pauline Baer de Perignon

TRANSLATED FROM THE FRENCH BY
NATASHA LEHRER

An Apollo Book

First published in French in 2020 as *La collection disparue*

First published in English in the US by New Vessel Press in 2022

First published in the UK in 2022 by Head of Zeus Ltd
This paperback edition first published in 2023 by Head of Zeus Ltd,
part of Bloomsbury Publishing Plc

9 7 5 3 1 2 4 6 8

A catalogue record for this book is available from the British Library.

ISBN (PB): 9781803280912
ISBN (E): 9781803280882

Printed and bound by CPI Group (UK) Ltd, Croydon, CR0 4YY

Head of Zeus Ltd
First Floor East
5–8 Hardwick Street
London EC1R 4RG

WWW.HEADOFZEUS.COM

In memory of my father, Philippe Baer
For my children, Elie, Rose, and Colombe
For Henri

TABLE OF CONTENTS

When it comes to art, only one thing counts: the pursuit of truth.
Errare humanum est!
But I plead good faith.
Jules Strauss, January 1931

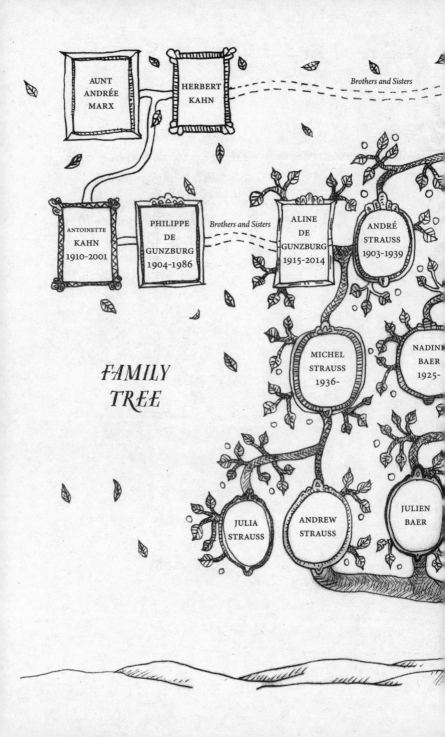

FAMILY TREE

AUNT ANDRÉE MARX

HERBERT KAHN

Brothers and Sisters

ANTOINETTE KAHN 1910-2001

PHILIPPE DE GUNZBURG 1904-1986

Brothers and Sisters

ALINE DE GUNZBURG 1915-2014

ANDRÉ STRAUSS 1903-1939

MICHEL STRAUSS 1936-

NADINE BAER 1925-

JULIA STRAUSS

ANDREW STRAUSS

JULIEN BAER

I

TREASURES OF THE PAST

If I close my eyes, I see walls hung with paintings. Portraits of lords and ladies of the eighteenth-century court rub shoulders with Degas's dancers, Monet's glowing landscapes, Sisley's snow-covered gardens.

There's a man standing there. He's been waiting for me a long time.

His eyes are smiling behind his small round spectacles. His face looks familiar, though I've never met him before. He has the same narrow moustache as my father, and wears white spats over his shoes.

He welcomes me into his study, where he talks me through each painting, describing the grace of a ballerina doing up the ribbon of her slipper, or the celestial beauty of an umbrella pine silhouetted against a blue sky. His voice fills with excitement as he tells the story of each picture, who painted it, where he came across it, what made him choose it.

I listen with such awe that he invites me to follow him, and escorts me to his apartment, through a vast gallery filled with pieces of art, bronze sculptures, and terracotta figures. It's dizzying, I can't take it all in. All of a sudden he turns, snatches up the fedora perched on the terracotta head of a comely young girl, and takes my arm. His wife calls out to him from afar, but he doesn't reply.

We step over three cairn terriers that the housekeeper has taken out for a walk and, laughing, run down the five flights of stairs of this beautiful Haussmann building on Avenue Foch.

Outside the chauffeur is waiting for him at the wheel of a sedan. Jules smiles at him but doesn't stop. The eagle carved into the stone façade of the building eyes us as we walk away down the side alley.

Jules lights a cigarette with the tip of the one he's just smoked. It's spring, the birds are singing, the sun is shining, and galleries await. Jacques Seligmann, Paul Rosenberg, the brothers Bernheim: Jules is warmly welcomed by his friends, his colleagues, dealers—all, like him, pioneers and lovers of impressionist art.

He looks like he's simply idling, but nothing escapes him.

He takes my hand and places it on a painting. Delicately, with the tips of his fingers, he shows me how to lightly touch the canvas to appreciate its texture.

Time and again, I conjure up this impossible meeting with my great-grandfather.

On a bookshelf in the drawing room of the apartment where I was born, sat an old, dust-covered book. I never noticed it was there, so of course I had no idea it contained images of the Impressionist paintings that made up my great-grandfather's collection. It had never once occurred to me to open the catalog of the "Private Sale, Jules Strauss Collection, 1932."

I could have asked my father to tell me about Jules Strauss, but I never did. My father died when I was twenty, before I was bold enough to ask him about the war, about his parents and grandparents, about his emotions and his memories.

On my aunt Nadine's—my father's sister's—desk, in the apartment in which she has lived for over sixty years, sits a small black-and-white photograph of an old man, his melancholy expression concealed behind his round spectacles. He has neatly combed gray hair, and a flannel suit that hangs a little loose. How many times has she mentioned her grandfather, while I barely listened, her words like background music scarcely to be heeded?

Those who could have told me things have long since died, and the questions I was never able to ask have disappeared with them.

And then one day, I have no idea why, quite out of the blue, the past suddenly resurfaced.

May 2014. My first encounter of true consequence with Jules Strauss was at a concert of Brazilian music. What was the connection between Caetano Veloso's "Cucurrucucu Paloma" and my great-grandfather Jules, who died in 1943? There was none, and I still can't explain why he popped into my life at that very moment.

I was sitting by the window, watching the rain. My daughters were bickering, and I should have been getting ready for the concert my husband, Henri, and I had been invited to. I was worn out from not having managed to write a word all day, and I couldn't get my daughters to stop squabbling. I needed an excuse to cancel.

But the temptation to dispel my gloomy mood, to escape the house, the rain, the shouting, pushed me out of the front door. *I'm on my way, Ipanema!* I pulled on an old velvet jacket that made me look like an eternal student, kissed Rose and Colombe goodbye, and grabbed a taxi to the Grand Rex.

Inside the concert hall, which was still virtually empty, I spotted my friend Alexis Kugel, an antique dealer with a passion for bossa nova, who'd invited us to the concert. He was deep in conversation, and from a distance the contrast between his stocky frame and the tall, rangy figure he was talking to made me smile. I thought about trying to slink past them to take my seat without being seen—I don't like interrupting conversations—but Alexis saw me and beckoned me over.

"Pauline! How are you? Allow me to introduce you to Andrew."

Andrew and I looked at each other and grinned like a couple of children sharing a secret. People were beginning to arrive, and they jostled past us as they made their way to their seats, but we remained standing where we were, delighted at the coincidence of meeting like this.

"But we already know each other!" said Andrew, in his strongly accented French.

Andrew is my elegant fifty-five-year-old cousin on my father's side. English-born, he's lived in France for thirty years without shedding his native accent. I hadn't set eyes on him for twenty years. His hair was beginning to go gray, and his face was a little gaunter than I recalled, but I recognized his distinctive physique, accent, and presence as soon as I saw him. I felt as though this chance encounter was a tiny sign from my deceased father.

"You're also a Caetano fan, are you? I've never missed a single one of his concerts."

Andrew showed me the little video camera he was planning to use to film the concert. He seemed to be with a gorgeous young woman who looked like she could be a model. I fiddled with the buttons on my dated old jacket, surprised that Andrew barely addressed a word to her and didn't bother to introduce us. He was too busy playing with the settings of his video camera.

"What are you up to nowadays?" he asked.

I knew perfectly well he was just being polite and wasn't really interested, but nonetheless I felt flustered. The last time I'd seen him I was eighteen, and he had been kind enough to offer me an internship at Sotheby's, the auction house where he still works. My job was to cut out and glue down photographs of paintings being put up for auction. This was before the Internet, and I'd found the work thankless and repetitive.

What had become of me twenty years on? I was writing, though I had yet to publish anything. I mentored others, hoping they would be more successful than I was. I didn't want to be nothing more than a full-time mother. I was looking for inspiration, trying to pluck up the confidence to do more with my life.

"I've got three children, and I run creative writing workshops. And . . . I write a little too."

I tried to make my voice sound confident and hoped he wouldn't ask me any more questions. Fortunately, he was no longer listening, being entirely absorbed by the concert, which had just begun. He was bewitched by Caetano's performance, but I'd soon had enough. I felt none of the magic of the bossa nova I loved. Caetano was playing bass guitar and I found it far too loud.

After a few more songs I had to resign myself to the fact that Caetano wasn't planning to play any of his big hits. I'd have been quite happy to leave, but Andrew seemed to think I was as much a fan as he, and I didn't want to bring the sudden and unexpected revival of our relationship to an abrupt end.

I was sitting with my hands discreetly trying to block my ears, when my cousin leaned toward me and said, with no preamble,

"Did you know there was something shady about the Strauss sale?"

Had I heard right? I wasn't sure I knew what he was talking about. The two words, "Strauss sale," echoed in my head for a long moment. It was as though a light in a tiny, neglected corner of my mind, filled with long-forgotten memories, was flickering to life. The words triggered something that preceded the actual memory of what they evoked.

What was Jules Strauss, our great-grandfather, doing showing up in the middle of this concert? Deafened by the music and completely thrown by Andrew bringing up his name, I wasn't sure if I should respond, or act as if I hadn't heard. Though I found the past resurfacing in such an unlikely setting very strange, a moment later curiosity got the better of me.

"Sorry? What do you mean, shady?"

Andrew continued talking, without taking his eyes off Caetano. I don't know if it was the earsplitting music or the shock of his revelation, but what he went on to say was indistinct. A miscellany of Degas's dancers, our great-grandfather Jules Strauss, auctions, Nazis, buyers, dummy companies, inventories.

Andrew's words sent my mind tumbling down a rabbit hole: I couldn't tell if the effect was pleasant, bizarre, or anxiety-inducing. I knew Jules Strauss had sold his collection of Impressionist paintings, but here was Andrew querying the circumstances of the sale, even saying something about the Nazis. Of course, Jules was Jewish! I'd never really thought about that before. The fragments of family history Andrew evoked were profoundly unsettling.

That was how Jules came back into my life. I was so taken aback I couldn't even think what to ask. I couldn't see

Caetano Veloso, I couldn't hear anything anymore, I was so thrown by this reconnection with the grandfather I had never known.

As the audience stood for the finale, I yelled in Andrew's ear:

"I don't understand, what was it that was so shady about the Strauss auction?"

"I think Jules was robbed," Andrew replied.

I didn't stand up and sing along with the rest of the audience for the finale. I had lost all interest in Caetano by that point. My mind was back in 1932. How stupid I was not to have asked my father anything before he died. Now the questions kept coming.

"Robbed? By whom, exactly? I don't understand."

But Andrew had left his seat and was edging closer to the stage so he could get a close-up of his idol. I waited for the end of the song before I got up to follow him. He looked so happy, filming the singer as he took his curtain call and the audience whooped and cheered.

"Did you know my daughter's named Victoria Caetana?"

I followed him up to the edge of the stage, clutching my jacket under my arm, my hair, which had been pinned up, now tumbling about my shoulders. I had so many questions. He handed me his business card.

"Call me. I'll explain."

Caetano launched into yet another encore. I pushed through the crowd toward the exit, deep in thought, and left the concert hall without saying goodbye to Alexis or Andrew. My husband caught up with me, intrigued to know what had happened. I couldn't respond to his questions. I wanted to linger for a moment in the distant, mysterious world of my family.

After we got home, I did my best to recount to Henri the snippets of information I'd grasped. He kept making me repeat myself, asking me questions to help me put what I'd managed to understand in order. Basically, Andrew had found a list of paintings that our family had declared stolen during the Second World War—the same paintings that Jules Strauss was supposed to have sold at auction in 1932. Andrew now suspected that the paintings had not in fact been sold.

"What are the paintings on Andrew's list?" Henri wanted to know.

"Degas, Renoir, Monet . . . I'm not sure. Andrew does. Selling Impressionist and modern paintings is the family business. I'm sure he knows what he's talking about."

I should have asked more questions, but I wasn't able to work up the courage. Overcome by the incongruity of the situation, I didn't have the presence of mind to prod Andrew for more details. I thought about my father: What had he known about his grandfather, and why had he never spoken of him?

Henri collects everything he can that relates to one of his ancestors, a French field marshal. Busts, portraits, commemorative china, even livery buttons with the family coat of arms. He loves history and genealogy, and is fascinated by mine too. He asked me what I knew about my great-grandfather. I thought he'd been born in Germany, but I couldn't remember either the precise place or date, and I'd never heard anyone speaking German during my childhood. He was a well-known art collector who was forced to sell his Impressionist paintings, "just one of which would have been worth a fortune today," according to the oft-repeated phrase at family gatherings. He'd been obliged to sell his collection in order to help his ruined brothers-in-law. I think, reading between the lines, that's why we almost never see my cousins on my father's side.

Every family has its paradise lost. The central figure in mine is Jules Strauss. Family legend has it that the auction of 1932, the details of which were never discussed, marked his downfall, the end of a golden age. The cursed sale toppled my family from their position as important and enlightened collectors, art world pioneers, to that of an ordinary, dull, bourgeois family occasionally visited by nostalgia for a vanished, glamorous world.

I remember as a child overhearing snatches of conversation about Renoir's "bathers," which Jules had been forced to sell, and what "they" would be worth today. I was struck with a sense of loss. At night, after I went to bed, I liked to fantasize about what our life might have been like if the collection hadn't been broken up and sold. But what is the point of regretting what one has never known? Eventually I chose to put it out of my mind.

Henri's eyes widened as I told him the little I knew about Jules Strauss. He opened my laptop and entered "Jules Strauss sale" in the search box. I didn't think for a moment that we'd find any trace of a man who had died seventy years earlier. But I was wrong: copies of the "Strauss Sale" catalog were available on eBay. Not just the 1932 sale—there had been two others, one in 1949 and one in 1961.

"Let's buy them all!" said Henri.

A simple search for "Jules Strauss" brought up dozens of references, images of paintings we'd never seen, and articles in art magazines.

"Wait, you're going too quickly." I felt exhausted all of a sudden. I wanted Henri to stop. I'd look tomorrow, perhaps, when I was alone.

But Henri carried on. He soon found the year of Jules's death: 1943. I had no idea he'd died during the war.

"Was he deported?" Henri wanted to know.

"No, I've always heard he died of old age."

I was aware how much my response left out. After decades of silence, seeing these details appear on a screen in a matter of seconds felt too sudden, too abrupt. I begged Henri to leave it for the following day. But he kept going, excitedly tapping out "stolen Jewish art collections," and "Jewish collections during the Second World War." The number of results was dizzying; academic articles, newspaper articles, bibliographies, sites where you could search by name or the title of a painting. I was exhausted and desperate to go to bed, yes, but at the same time I was riveted, and couldn't keep my eyes off the screen.

Why had I never wondered how Jules Strauss, a Jewish art collector, had made it through the war?

"Looks like you've finally found your subject!" Henri knew I'd been wanting to write a book for years, and I still liked to think that one day I might. But this wasn't just any subject—this was my family, my history. I was exhausted and filled with trepidation. What secrets might I uncover? I wanted to go to bed and not talk about it anymore.

Some time after the concert Henri persuaded me to watch a documentary with him. "You'll need to take notes." He handed me a pen. I struggled to concentrate—as I always do when a subject is a little too close to the bone—while we watched Rachel Kahn's film *Nazi Plunder*, in which she follows three artworks that had belonged to Jewish collectors, from their theft by the Nazis to their return to their original owners' families. Matisse's *Femme assise* (*Seated Woman*), from the collection of the great art dealer Paul Rosenberg, had been spotted in a photograph that showed Hermann Göring picking out paintings at the Jeu de Paume in Paris, by an eagle-eyed art historian named Emmanuelle Polack. I sat up now, alert. Henri was insistent: she was the person I had to call. But I wasn't quite ready yet.

II

MEMORIES FOR SALE

January 2016. My aunt Nadine, leaning on her cane, was waiting for me by the front door of the family apartment. She had put on a pretty silk blouse and several strings of brightly colored beads in honor of my visit. As per our usual habit, I followed her as she made her way slowly toward the sitting room. I put on the lights to brighten the gloom, turned down the burning hot radiator, and switched off the television. Nadine offered me a cup of coffee, but I declined. I didn't want to tire her. We sat across from each other. My aunt had asked me over to entrust me with some earrings she was hoping to sell. She was ninety-one, and this was not the first time she'd had to worry about money. "I never thought I'd live this long," she said. I rejoiced at her longevity.

As she rummaged around in a cupboard for the jewelry she'd squirreled away, I wandered around the sitting room, where nothing had changed since the Sunday lunches of my childhood. I peered at the faded, yellowing pictures on the walls as if seeing them for the first time. Who was the woman whose beautiful portrait hung above the green sofa? Where did the yellow-and-blue paintings with Chinese motifs that hung over the dining table come from? I paused in front of the intricately carved wooden moldings on a pretty, slightly scratched Louis XV bureau. Was this all that remained of the Strauss family fortune?

Meanwhile Nadine had unearthed the jewelry. They weren't earrings but dress clips in the shape of shells, which women used to attach to their clothes like brooches. She'd been given them by her aunt Andrée, who had some kind of link with Suzanne Belperron, the avant-garde designer who had made them. Belperron made pieces for the Duchess of Windsor, and her jewelry is highly sought after by collectors nowadays. She took part in the resistance during the war, and when Bernard Herz, the jeweler for whom she worked, was deported, she did all she could to save the family and the business. I hadn't quite understood the link between Belperron and our family. "Belperron worked for Bernard Herz, and Aunt Andrée was Herz's sister-in-law," Nadine explained.

"Was Herz Jewish?"

"Of course. Everyone was Jewish," Nadine replied, laughing. What she meant was, "Everyone in our circle was Jewish."

I was much less interested in the history of Nadine's clips than in that of the Strausses. "Do you remember the auction that took place in 1932?" I asked.

"Pauline, I was seven. We were living with our grandparents, but they never spoke of such things in front of the children."

I pressed her. "But do you know what made Jules decide to sell his collection of Impressionist paintings?"

"His brothers-in-law were both ruined in the 1929 crash. My father also had all his money in the stock market. Which is why we moved in with my grandparents."

Her mother, my grandmother Élisabeth, had moved into her parents' large apartment at 60 Avenue Foch with her husband, Louis, and their two children, my father, Philippe, and his little sister Nadine. From a console table, I picked up a little framed black-and-white photo that showed an elderly couple standing on a cobbled street. It was an old photograph, and their features were a little out of focus. The man was tall, lean, and elegant, and the petite woman next to him was wearing a pretty hat.

"Is this Marie-Louise and Jules?" I asked. Nadine nodded.

"When was it taken?"

"Just before the war, I think."

"Where were they living in 1940? You'd already left Paris, but where were they?"

"They stayed behind in their apartment in Paris."

"But how did they escape the deportations?"

"Bon Papa was already old, you know."

How could I have spent two years coauthoring a documentary for French television about the Nuremberg trials, listening to and reading dozens of witness statements given by Nazi criminals and their victims, and never once cast doubt on the official version of my own family history, according to which, with the exception of one of Jules and Marie-Louise's sons-in-law, everyone had made it through the war unscathed?

That day was the first time I realized there was something about the story that didn't make sense. How had this wealthy Jewish couple, well-known art collectors, been able to stay in Paris, entirely untroubled by the Nazis, throughout the war? I realized I knew nothing about the people in the photograph, or anything of what they had been through together.

I suddenly remembered to tell her about bumping into Andrew. "Isn't that a funny coincidence!" I tried to keep my tone light. "He told me he thinks there was something shady about the 1932 auction. What do you make of that? Do you think Jules could have been robbed?"

Nadine lifted her shoulders in puzzlement. "What on earth? No, of course not."

I didn't insist. She was an old lady, and I didn't want to upset her, especially on the day she was parting with some jewelry that meant a great deal to her. Her father's financial ruin can't have been easy, but she never spoke of it. She preferred to reminisce about her childhood, being pampered by her grandfather in the luxurious surroundings of the apartment on Avenue Foch. She told me about the pony he had given her, and the chauffeur who took her to buy pastries every day after school.

I listened to her reminiscences as though to a familiar lullaby. Out of habit I flipped open a little silver box on the coffee table, which hadn't held candies for many years. On the wall opposite, half-hidden by a chaise longue, I spied a small oil painting of a naked woman lying in a field of flowers.

"The little painting over there is a Renoir, no?"

Nadine burst out laughing. "Well, kind of. It's a fake. The last time Michel, Andrew's father, was in Paris, he inspected it very carefully. And yes, it's still a fake!"

A few days later Nadine and I met up again, at the premises of an antique dealer who had published a monograph about Suzanne Belperron. He looked at the jeweled clips and made an offer, which Nadine immediately accepted. I suggested that she take a few hours to think about it, but the dealer was insistent. His impatience roused my suspicions. I tried to persuade my aunt to get another valuation, but she refused. I was furious with both the dealer and Nadine. We left, both of us unsettled by the meeting. I had the slightly uncomfortable feeling that it was almost inevitable that an old lady so obviously keen to sell was bound to be taken for a ride. I realized I was going to have to get another valuation.

A few days after that, alone this time, I made an appointment at Sotheby's to find out what Nadine's clips were worth. Sitting opposite the expert, who told me he found them very beautiful, I fell to thinking once more about their origins. Who was this aunt Andrée who was related to the famous Belperron? I didn't know that this detail of their history endowed the pieces with greater value. I called Nadine.

"Remind me how you're related to Aunt Andrée?"

"She was married to Herbert Kahn, my grandmother Marie-Louise's brother. When she died, she left me the clips in her will. She knew how much I liked them."

Nadine hadn't forgotten anything about these people whose names meant nothing to me. After the clips have been sold, once Nadine is no longer alive, what will remain of these memories? I wasn't very proud to be the niece flogging the family jewels, and I left the auction house in a melancholy frame of mind. I paused for a moment in the marble entrance hall and rummaged in my handbag for the business card that Andrew had handed me at the concert. "Call me, I'll explain," he'd said. I hesitated. This was the auction house where Andrew worked. I could have asked his advice, but I didn't want him to know that Aunt Nadine was selling her jewelry. Apart from anything else, I had no desire whatsoever to be the person whose imprudent dealings led to her depriving several generations of her family of their priceless treasures. Andrew's branch of the family had held on to its fortune and, aided by Jules's reputation, had kept the Strauss name alive, passing the baton as art world experts from father to son, all the while doubtless continuing to acquire valuable works of art, while our side of the family was forced to decide what to sell off.

But in Sotheby's chilly, opulent foyer, I began to consider a new option, as though in response to the anger and shame I'd been feeling since the visit to the Belperron specialist—that of getting back the vanished treasures that had once belonged to my family. This wild flight of fancy filled me with both resolve and hope. I wanted to be the dauntless knight in shining armor who recovered the family fortune and restored its honor.

The decision to call my cousin from the foyer that day marked the beginning of my investigation.

Andrew answered straightaway. He was still in his office, and he asked me to wait downstairs for him. A few minutes later he met me in the intimidating black marble-lined foyer. As he emerged from the elevator the first thing I noticed was how slim and elegant he looked in his dark tailored suit. He gave me a friendly smile. He was entirely at home here, and he sat down at the reception desk, which was unstaffed at the end of the working day.

"Andrew, you remember that time we met at the concert, you told me about some stolen paintings? I didn't really understand. It was so loud. Do you think you could explain it to me now?"

He picked up the receptionist's notepad and tore out a page. I watched as he scribbled down the details of the paintings that had been declared stolen. I was speechless. I may not have been an expert in art history, but I understood the significance of three by Degas, four Renoirs, two Sisleys, two Monets.

"Andrew, who filed the declaration that they had been stolen? When?"

I was no less stunned than the first time he'd told me. I still couldn't bring myself to ask him all the questions that flooded into my mind. I was filled with a mixture of apprehension and curiosity. It would have been easy enough for me to get up and leave, and never think about any of it again.

I'd already got involved, against my better judgement, with Nadine's financial problems, and I had no intention of getting caught up in old family business that went back two generations, let alone digging into wartime secrets about Nazi thefts.

I smiled at Andrew, though I really wanted to get up and run away. Keep your jewelry and your paintings and let me go home and be with my children!

But Jules was beckoning me. I saw him standing in the doorway and all of sudden I was struck with the realization that I could not turn away from him now.

III

THE AUCTION CATALOG

The first picture on Andrew's scribbled list was a pastel drawing by Degas, the *Portrait of Jacques de Nittis as a Child*.

A boy is leaning over the seat of an armchair, drawing. He is dressed somewhat eccentrically, in a short, pleated tartan kilt and striped leggings. He must be five or six years old. Drawn in profile, hair disheveled, bending over his picture, pencil in hand, he gives a charming impression of being both a little unkempt and deeply focused. He reminds me of my daughter Colombe, so concentrated when she is drawing that she is completely unaware of the world around her. I wonder if my great-grandfather was taken by the impression of suspended time in the drawing, the child in his imaginary world, observed by the adult, for whom nothing else exists but this beloved little boy.

There's a crumpled sheet of paper at the boy's feet. The beige and brown tones are lit up by what looks like a red tassel on his jacket, and a patch of blue behind a little figurine on a horse, a plaything that the child has placed on the arm of the chair.

I did an internet search for the drawing and it came up

immediately on my computer screen; only one Degas drawing of a little boy exists. It was harder to identify the other pictures whose titles Andrew had jotted down for me. When I searched for *Roses dans un vase* (*Roses in a Vase*) by Renoir, I found two dozen still lifes. As for Degas's *Danseuses sur des pointes* (*Dancers on Point*), I had no idea if this meant a group of dancers in pink or in blue. I found lots of portraits of young girls with ribbons in their hair, but not Renoir's *Jeune fille au ruban rouge* (*Young Girl with a Red Ribbon*). I needed more details. I needed to get hold of the catalog of the 1932 Strauss auction.

Apparently, my father had been so crazy about flea markets, he wanted to call me "Brocante" for the kind of objects he loved to find there. Every time I visit my childhood home, where my mother now lives alone, I'm reminded of his passion. Together, my parents built up a collection—rather more modest that Jules's of course—of hundreds of pieces of folk art. As long as I can remember, a majestic bronze statue that once belonged to Jules, of Louis XIV on horseback, garbed in the draped mantle of antiquity with a sword at his waist, has kept fond watch over an old brass compass, various modest works of art by friends, and a set of bronze polygons. When I was little, I was allowed to touch all these odd knickknacks, but I knew that the bronze horse was far more precious, and I only ever touched its smooth, polished surface in secret. One day I tried to see if this horse that served no purpose had moving parts, which would have made it much more fun. I unhooked Louis XIV's sword, then quickly refastened it to his belt, my heart beating. I didn't get caught.

A few days after Andrew gave me the list of paintings, I went to visit my mother to find out what she knew. Amused by my sudden curiosity, she took down from a shelf a dust-covered brochure that my father had kept there—the 1932 sale catalog that somehow I'd never noticed before.

I leafed through the pages in silence, impressed by the names of the artists and marveling at the paintings of dancers, bathers, spring vistas, and snow-covered landscapes whose styles and motifs I recognized. Though I knew nothing about them, I nonetheless understood that these were masterpieces. I was no longer in my father's overflowing library, but in the great light-filled galleries of a museum, wandering among remarkable works by Degas, Renoir, Vuillard, and Boudin.

Were the numbers jotted down in the margin the estimated value or the sale price of each work? My mother didn't recognize the handwriting.

"I found this for you too," she said, handing me two more catalogs: *Strauss Sale 1949* and *Strauss Sale 1961*.

As I flicked through them, I discovered dozens of seventeenth- and eighteenth-century paintings. Some were by Italian painters, including Rubens and Titian, but most were French—Watteau, Fragonard, Pater. There were images of antique furniture, silverware, and porcelain. I had not the remotest idea how much these treasures might be worth. How was it that my father had never mentioned these catalogs to me? "What do you know about Jules Strauss?" I asked my mother. "What did Papa tell you about him?"

"He was the family patriarch, the man your father admired more than anyone else—for his intelligence and kindness, his culture and his curiosity. He used to take your father to museums and to visit antique dealers."

I couldn't help wondering why, if Jules was so important to my father, he'd never talked to us about him.

"Was he upset by the sale of family heirlooms, the loss of this collection?" I wondered.

"No, he was far too intelligent for that," she said. "Your father liked books and writers more than painters. Jules gave him several lavishly illustrated books when he was a child. The only writer Jules cared for was Balzac." I recalled that toward the end of his life, my father had bought himself the entire set of *The Human Comedy*, which he used to read every summer.

My mother was born in Toulouse in 1940, at almost exactly the same time my father left Paris for the Free Zone. I asked her if Papa had ever talked to her about the war, or at least more than he did to his children.

"Very little, and only to tell me the odd anecdote or funny story. He was a radio operator in General Leclerc's Second Armored Division, and sometimes, apparently, he was so nervous and trembling so badly, he couldn't tap out the Morse code. And during the Normandy landings, he sat on his glasses and broke them!"

These were stories I already knew. I smiled, but my heart wasn't in it. I simply could not believe my father's silence was a mere matter of modesty and discretion.

IV

THE PHANTOM OF THE MUSEUM

I can spend hours at my desk in the little ground floor, glass-walled studio I rent for the writing workshops I run, far from the house and the children, gazing through the windows at the deep pink camelia flowers that bloom sometimes as early as February. I knew I should be planning my new workshops, but I was out of ideas, and I didn't even have a starting date in mind. All I could think about were the ten pictures on Andrew's list. I pinned photocopies all over the walls.

The pictures on Andrew's list were in the 1932 catalog. Despite the yellowing paper, and even though the photograph is in black-and-white, Monet's *Les Pins Parasols, Cap d'Antibes* (*Stone Pines, Cap d'Antibes*) glows. I was dazzled by the simplicity of the composition, the row of pines with the sky and the sea behind, the beauty of the light and the colors, the landscape's impression of deep tranquility. It conjured the same emotion that the Mediterranean coast summons in me, the blue sky after the mistral drops, the familiar road between Vidauban and La Garde-Freinet in the Var, that cuts through the red earth of southern France, the sway of the pines floating like deep green clouds. It didn't take long to find out that the painting is now in a private collection.

Le Départ de la course (*The Start of the Race*), by Degas, also known as *The Riders*, is in the collection of the National Gallery of Art in Washington. On the museum's website I found some skimpy details of the painting's genealogy, passing straight from Jules Strauss (1932) to Paul Mellon (1950), the great benefactor of the museum, to which he donated his personal collection.

What made Andrew suspect these paintings had been stolen? Where did his list come from? He was familiar with the art market, and I wondered why he hadn't solved the riddle himself, indeed why he'd even mentioned it to me. I know next to nothing about art history or painting. What a shame I hadn't picked anything up when I'd worked for Andrew all those years ago. I'd barely glanced at the images as I glued them onto index cards. Now I was absolutely desperate to find out as much as I could about the paintings in Jules's collection.

I tried to talk to Andrew again, but he was too busy to respond to all my questions, so I decided it was time to begin researching. I started with the websites of the museums where the paintings are held today. The walls of my office gradually filled up with reproductions of paintings and Post-its covered in scrawled questions and possible leads. I'm not good at remembering names and dates, but I love riddles and mysteries. I was learning and taking everything in at speed, as if some of Jules's curiosity had been passed on to me. This sudden interest was not only linked to a belated interest in art.

More than the pictures themselves, I was interested in their histories, how they had passed from one owner to another and traversed different eras.

But to find out about the life of a painting, you need more than the Internet. Since I was doing research into Impressionist art, I set out for the Musée d'Orsay to continue my detective work.

At a discreet side entrance on rue de Lille used only by employees and researchers, all I needed to do was show my identity card to gain entrance to the documentation center and the museum's library. I made my way past the crowd of visitors, along a small lateral walkway that crosses the main gallery inside the former railway station. I didn't so much as glance at the wonderful paintings by Courbet, or the Rodin sculptures, or the magnificent clock on the great glass wall. I reached a door that was out of sight of the public and knocked to gain entrance to the inner sanctum that contains the archives, the indispensable but hidden part of the museum's holdings. A further identity check, then I got in the elevator that goes down to the museum reserves in the basement and up to the curators' offices, all the way at the top of the building. The fourth floor—modern, a little chilly, the floors covered in synthetic carpet—houses the two departments that interested me, that is, the library and the documentation center, where I randomly decided to begin: a long corridor with small rooms like alcoves leading off it, the walls lined with shelves of brown boxes.

Apart from the magnificent view over the Seine, the place is simple, modest, its scale human. You can almost smell the accretion of documents, the lack of space, the dust, and the scholarship. I immediately spotted a sign above a wall of shelves marked "Degas," with archive boxes labeled "Solo dancers," "Rehearsals," "Groups of dancers in pink" and "Blue dancers." I wanted to rush right over and open them up so I could look inside.

"Madame, do you have your reader's card?"

I'd walked right past the entrance desk. The dark-haired woman sitting behind it beckoned me over. Anyone is permitted to access the boxes of documents, provided they register and can justify their research.

"What's your subject?" the woman asked.

"Degas, Renoir, Monet . . . "

She looked at me skeptically. It was a bit vague. There must be hundreds of people doing research on these painters. I decided to admit that I wasn't a student.

"I'm doing some research on my great-grandfather."

She still looked doubtful; I wondered whether family history was an authorized area of study. I was beginning to worry she wasn't going to let me in.

"His name was Jules Strauss." At this, her face lit up.

"Jules Strauss the collector?"

Clearly all that's needed is to know the password! Thank you, Jules, I would never have guessed your name wielded such power. I felt like dancing down the corridor. Without waiting for her to finish, I rushed over to the "collectors' boxes," large brown canvas archival boxes stacked on shelves near the entrance, handwritten names on the labels. Excitedly, I grabbed the box labeled "Strauss—Strauss." And as if the documents had been waiting for me forever, inside I found a fat folder labeled "Jules Strauss. "Don't forget the *fantôme!*" the woman said, handing me a large piece of cardboard. A fantôme, or phantom, is how the library referred to the flat card that acts as a placeholder when a folder is removed from a box.

I drew out a thick cardboard sleeve labeled *Jules Strauss* and opened it. My first surprise: I had no idea that his collection had been so extensive. Many more Impressionist works had passed through his hands than the ones listed in the 1932 auction catalog. Between 1890 and 1930 he'd bought dozens of pictures by Degas, Monet, Renoir, and Sisley.

Inside the folder was another sleeve labeled *1902 Sale*. Over the two decades after his arrival in Paris from Frankfurt, Jules built up a remarkable collection of Impressionist paintings, including seventeen by Alfred Sisley. Sisley had only begun to be appreciated in 1899, with the success of a posthumous sale of his work organized by his friend Claude Monet.

In the introduction to the 1902 catalog, Arsène Alexandre, a well-known critic at the time who specialized in Sisley's oeuvre, extols the beauty of the collection: "Nowhere else have I seen a selection as accomplished, unusual, and complete," he writes. "The owner of this collection has brought together a number of particularly delicate notes, exquisite harmonies of subtlety and light. Marvelous skies, views of villages, limpid pools, sketches of Louveciennes, [. . .], nothing is lacking for the person who wishes to discover and appreciate Sisley." And then this paean to Jules himself:

"Overall, this collection reveals a man of exquisite taste who sets store by quality rather than quantity. The Strauss sale will go down as a major event in the history of Impressionism and modern art. When a carefully put-together collection like this is put up for sale, it is as though one is witnessing the dispersal of an entire education." A newspaper article from the time noted that as a result of the sale Jules was dubbed "Monsieur Sisley."

Inside another sleeve were papers pertaining to the 1932 sale, but there was nothing there that wasn't in the catalog. Between the two sales, Jules seems to have purchased at least thirty works by Degas and as many Renoirs. A few paintings by Delacroix, too, and a Courbet—the list grew longer, and my list of questions too. I filled my notebook with jumbled notes, took three photographs of each document—I couldn't believe my eyes, and I needed evidence that it was all real, that I wasn't dreaming. Was my great grandfather really one of the first great collectors of Impressionist art? Had he known these painters during their lifetimes? I wondered how he'd developed this taste, how he had discovered these artists and learned to appreciate them, this man who had been barely twenty years old when he arrived in Paris from Germany. And the biggest puzzle of all—what had become of Jules's masterpieces?

V

ON THE TRAIL OF JULES

Every day at opening time, I would enter the Musée d'Orsay through the side door, the researchers' entrance, show my identity card, and position a sticker marked "visitor" on my coat lapel. I particularly liked Mondays, when the museum was closed to the public and it felt like I had the place to myself. I'd hurry along the walkway, across the echoing silence of the main gallery, impatient to walk through the discreet little door that led into a hidden world. Behind the scenes at the museum.

I would leave my bag in a locker and take the elevator up to the fourth floor. The lady at the entrance to the documentation center knew me by now, and always greeted me with a little smile as she handed me a fantôme. I would climb the stepladder and bring down boxes of index cards to look through. Since the reproductions in the catalogs were of such poor quality, she suggested I look for better ones in the adjacent library.

Here, once again, Jules's name was my open sesame. As soon as I uttered it, the librarian snapped to attention. Without missing a beat, she asked,

"Do you think your great-grandfather's collection was looted by the Nazis?"

I wasn't shocked by the directness of her question. She was simply articulating the hypothesis that I had up till that point not dared to formulate out loud.

"Maybe. I don't know."

"Wait a minute." She picked up a piece of paper and a pen, and we both went and sat down at a table in the reading room, which was otherwise empty.

This beautiful woman with shimmering eyeshadow was called Helena Patsiamanis. Her name was Greek, but she had a German accent. She wore rather severe spectacles, but behind them her eyes were kind. She told me she had put together a selection of books on looted art and created a new section for them in the library with its own classification. Listening to her, I couldn't help wondering if this dark period of history might have touched her own family. I admitted to her that I didn't have any real idea of what I was looking for, and that I was fairly uninformed not only about art but also about the modus operandi of the Nazi art thieves.

Methodically, she asked me a few questions and took notes. She wanted to know who Jules's friends were, what art dealers he knew, anything I knew about his habits and his relationships, and if he had any particular character traits.

Since I was unable to answer these questions, Helena suggested I interview members of the family and record our conversations. She told me to look for papers and photographs at my aunt and uncles' apartments. And of course, I was going to have to read everything I could lay my hands on about the world of prewar Jewish collectors.

"You need to sketch a psychological portrait of Jules Strauss. Try to find out as much as you can about him, his personality, his taste, the kind of man he was. It's the only way to get a sense of how he would have reacted to what happened during the war, the kinds of decisions he might have taken."

The rigor of her approach took me by surprise. Who would be able to tell me anything about Jules, given that he had died over seventy years earlier? I thought about my father's cousins whom I never saw. I was going have to gather my courage to talk to them.

"You're going to become a detective, following the trail of your family's history. Every detail counts."

"But I'm not a private detective!" I pictured a wall covered in photographs, string, and little flags, like you see in police procedural movies. Helena seemed serious. She suggested I begin with Andrew's list, explaining that I would need to establish the provenance of each picture, in other words the history and journey of the piece, from when it was painted, right up to the present day. When and how it had changed hands from one owner, one collector, one dealer to the next. It was this journey, this genealogy, that I was going to have to trace as precisely as possible. I think I'd already begun to do this even before I came across the term "provenance."

I discovered there was a thing called a *catalogue raisonné*, an exhaustive inventory of the entire body of an artist's work.

Impatiently, I worked my way through the four fat volumes containing details of every picture Degas ever painted. In the index I discovered the name of my great-grandfather. The Strauss collection was growing; Jules had owned over twenty of Degas's works.

My astonishment was followed immediately by incomprehension. Why had my father never told me about any of this, or taken me to museums to see these paintings?

I followed Helena's advice, and discovered that the *Portrait of Jacques de Nittis as a Child* had twice been put up for sale by Jules Strauss, first in 1902, and for a second time in 1932.

Was this an element of the psychological profile that Helena had spoken of? Had he bought and sold according to his financial situation, or because his tastes had changed?

I confided my bafflement to Helena: If these works had been sold by Strauss in 1932, how could they subsequently have been stolen from him? She thought it was possible they hadn't been sold in 1932, but "bought in." The term is used either for a painting that has failed to find a buyer at auction, or has for some reason been withdrawn from the sale. This would mean that though it was listed in the 1932 catalog, Degas's *Portrait* might have remained in the Strauss collection.

Nadine was getting used to me calling her three times a day with questions about the family or the paintings. I called her now and asked, with no introductory explanation,

"Nadine, do you remember a picture called *Portrait of Jacques de Nittis as a Child*?"

The name meant nothing to her, but when I described the little schoolboy, drawn from behind by Degas, the memories came flooding back.

"Oh yes, it hung on the wall above your father's bed, in the apartment on Avenue Foch."

"Did you see it again after the war? In the Avenue Foch apartment, or somewhere else, maybe at Marie-Louise's? Do you know if they kept it?"

Nadine paused for a moment. "I don't think so, no. It must have been sold."

I imagined myself entering my father's childhood bedroom, under the amused eye of Jules, gazing with affection at his two little schoolboys. I wondered if Jules had bought the picture because it reminded him of his grandson. Might he have purchased it a third time before the war? Had it, as Helena suggested, simply not found a buyer in 1932, or been withdrawn from the sale? Was it possible that the same had happened with the other pictures on Andrew's list?

A strange theory popped into my head: Had Jules Strauss been the secret purchaser of the pictures he sold in 1932, which the Nazis later stole from him?

VI

THE SECRETS OF A COLLECTOR

"I'm the collector of collectors," Alexis Kugel told me, as we sat drinking coffee one morning in the café where we'd agreed to meet after I dropped the children off at school.

I've known Alexis, a warm and generous-hearted man, for several years. He loves to sing and play the piano, and has a constant stream of visitors to his apartment, which is filled with stunning, unusual, and valuable objects, an extension of the gallery he owns on the floor below. It's like a palace of wondrous works, for sale at prices I dare not ask. I don't find him intimidating, because he is such a lovely, generous man, filled with joie de vivre. It's a delight to listen to him describing the latest things he's unearthed, medieval goblets or a ceremonial chain of the Order of the Golden Fleece. I sometimes suspect that he prefers the company of objects and their mysteries to that of other people.

Heir to a dynasty of antique dealers—he was only nineteen when he and his brother took over the gallery after their father's untimely death—he's knowledgeable about all eras, with a particular interest in French and European art of the seventeenth and eighteenth centuries. I was a little taken aback to discover that he knew more about my great-grand-father than I did.

"Strauss was typical of the Jewish collectors of the day," he told me. "He loved French eighteenth-century art, and he had a pronounced taste for the French Regency style, which he helped popularize among the Parisian bourgeoisie. He loved unusual objects with a history—following in the tradition of cabinets of curiosities. He was part of the third wave of collectors of Impressionist art, which he began acquiring at studio sales in 1890. Unfortunately, he sold a little too early."

Alexis had brought with him catalogs of the three Strauss sales from his personal archive. He believed a catalog told you everything about a collector, as some people think a book does about its author. I found myself holding my great-grandfather's three volume œuvre.

"He was what I like to call a horizontal collector, meaning that he only bought things he loved, in any genre. They had to be special in some way, whatever their monetary value. He sought out unusual pieces of French Regency-era furniture, ornaments, and drawings. He always preferred an unusual sketch to something flashy, fancy, and obvious. And he loved to live among his accumulated treasures, among works of art that made his life beautiful. He enjoyed showing them off, as opposed to the kind of collector who likes to squirrel them away. I'd contrast him with the vertical collector, who focuses on one area in an obsessive way, with no interest in anything else, like the collector of sublime Saxon porcelain who lives in an apartment furnished entirely from Ikea."

I loved this image of Jules living with his art, always on the lookout for something unusual and beautiful, not doing it for show. Alexis showed me his father's notes in the margins of the 1961 catalog. Then he read me the catalog's preface by Jacques Dupont, who was then president of the Friends of the Louvre: "The collection never stopped growing and, during the terrible years of the Occupation, it was a difficult task to keep all these objects safe. Distraught in the wake of his son's death, harried by persecution, devastated by the tragedy that had befallen his country, Jules Strauss died in 1943."

The allusion in Dupont's words was striking: "Persecution . . . the tragedy that had befallen his country." Dupont was clearly tacitly referring to the Occupation and the Nazi persecution of the Jews.

"Be careful, you mustn't burn your wings," Alexis warned me. "This kind of research can take years and become an obsession. It will take much longer and be much more difficult than you think, with no guarantee of success. And there's the risk of uncovering unpleasant surprises, and even getting into family disputes."

He suggested that we go down to the gallery. He had something he wanted to show me. A few minutes later I was seated at his desk, and he brought over a small eighteenth-century box made of laquered ebony, decorated with Chinese-style flowers and landscapes. It reminded me of the paintings in Nadine's apartment, the chinoiserie that had been so fashionable in Jules's time.

I opened it and carefully took out one of the four large, surprisingly solid, white porcelain cups nestled inside, adorned with small Chinese figures in red and gold and rimmed with gold leaf.

"In fact they aren't cups, they're containers for cosmetics. And it's not real Chinese lacquer, but *Vernis Martin*, an imitation that was very fashionable at the time. This was exactly the kind of thing your great-grandfather liked. He collected soft paste porcelain, which is particularly fine and fragile."

"Would it be indiscreet to ask you how you acquired them?"

"Not at all. I bought them from Antoinette de Gunzbourg about twenty years ago."

I was very fond of my aunt Antoinette de Gunzbourg, the daughter of Aunt Andrée, of the Belperron clips. She was warm and free-spirited, and gave me English lessons, rolling her *R*s in her strong French accent.

I realized Alexis knew my entire family, which gave me a strange, even slightly disagreeable feeling. I was disappointed that I couldn't buy back this little box. I didn't own a single thing that had belonged to Jules, not even a tiny memento, and it seemed like everyone else knew more about him than I did. I left Alexis's gallery in a state of emotional exhaustion. Perhaps one day I would no longer have to ask another person to tell me about my great-grandfather.

VII

SKETCH

After my fortuitous meeting with Andrew, it was as if a machine had started in my head, generating an endless sequence of questions that led only to more questions. The long list of chores to do with the children and the apartment was replaced by lists of paintings to be located, books to read, experts to contact. I raced from archive to archive, filling dozens of notebooks with notes and references. I sent emails to historians, professors, and museum curators. I met an academic who specializes in the study of prewar, bourgeois Jewish families and was familiar with every detail of the Strauss and Gunzbourg family trees. He explained that within these banking families who had moved to Paris from Frankfurt and Vienna, the cousins would all marry one another. I began an enthralling correspondence with Marc Masurovsky, an American historian and cofounder of the Holocaust Art Restitution Project, who guided me through the archives and helped me with the more arcane details of the way the Gestapo operated. I interviewed descendants of well-known collectors. I discovered that some couldn't even bear for the subject to be mentioned, while others were fascinated by the most insignificant stories about their families. I spoke to everyone I could, pursued every available lead, came up with a thousand theories. I would get up in the middle of the night to write down some thought that had occurred to me as I drifted off to sleep; in the morning I would fire off emails filled with questions, and in the afternoon I'd return to one or other of the archives. I got to the point where I couldn't talk about anything else. I discussed everything in the most minute detail with various members of the family. They listened patiently, sensing my overwhelming urge to share. With each new discovery, I'd call my brother Julien:

"Did you know that Jules owned more than five hundred paintings, and I haven't even finished going through the list? Have you any idea how much Monet's *Charing Cross Bridge* would be worth today?"

We laughed about the Lamborghini he was going to buy himself if I ever located the painting. It was a private joke, a tactful means for my solicitous older brother to check on how my research was going. He knew me well, recognized my fluctuating moods and my tendency to lose heart, and always encouraged me to keep going.

Charing Cross Bridge, which now hangs in the Museo Thyssen-Bornemisza in Madrid, sold for $4 million in 1996. I walked around for a few days thinking I was a millionaire, until I realized that Jules had sold it in 1926, a few months before Monet's death. Too bad. I soldiered on. A friend gave me the phone number of a collector familiar with the Strauss collection. He was the son of friends of my grandparents. They had lived in a beautiful apartment looking onto the Parc Monceau. Nadine remembered going there as a child. She told me the father had a wonderful sense of humor. After several failed attempts to speak on the phone, I at last managed to get hold of the son, but I found him a little cold, as if I was disturbing him. He had very few memories of my family, just a vague recollection of Nadine as a child. No memory of the apartment on Avenue Foch. He said it was because he had been too young at the time, but I rather got the feeling he did not want to remember anything that day. "It was my parents who were friends of your grandparents." I tried to ask him a few more questions, but without success. And then right at the end of the conversation, he said,

"My father was deported."

I felt terrible to have bothered him. How could I have forgotten how lucky we had been? I hoped he would forgive me.

I still went almost daily to the Musée d'Orsay, arriving in the morning just as it opened. I would greet Helena and go through all the questions that had germinated during the night in my febrile mind. I was making real headway, far more than in anything I'd ever done before. It was as if, after a long silence, the information was just there, waiting to be uncovered. It seemed within my grasp—in the same way that, after years of trying to write, once I began to tell the story of my hunt for the truth, the words I'd spent so many years fumbling for began to come to me at last. My memories, my feelings, everything that mattered to me, all the things I wanted to say but was never able to formulate—finally it was all taking shape. I was finding my voice.

My research into the provenance of *Portrait of Jacques de Nittis as a Child* led me to Sergei Shchukin, the great Russian collector of modern and Impressionist art, whose collection is today split between the Hermitage Museum in St. Petersburg and the Pushkin State Museum of Fine Arts in Moscow. Jules bought the pastel from him in 1900. In 1914, he went to visit Shchukin at his Moscow mansion, which the collector had recently opened to the public. He recounted the visit to Marie-Louise in a letter that Nadine gave me to read, in which he described Shchukin and his son:

> The father is a true art lover, literally stammering with delight as he showed me around his treasures. He knows Paris very well. He used to live near the Gobelins tapestry manufactory, in the 13th arrondissement. We gathered very simply in the dining room around a samovar.
>
> This morning we were shown around the mansion, with its grand courtyard and garden, the staircase with two large panels by Matisse, the huge drawing room with four Degas, six Monets, Sisleys, Pissarros etc. Then another drawing room with three incredible Renoirs, a Cézanne, a sublime Degas nude. I was allowed to wander freely, and believe me when I say I did! Then the music room, with twenty Matisses, what an extraordinary

effect, for him they're flowers on a carpet, whatever you want them to be, I didn't quite follow, to be honest, but I could see that the effect was startling, raw. Anarchic. Then the dining room with twenty fabulous Gauguins, absolutely glorious, and finally his bedroom, where there are only Picassos, he prefers their grand simplicity, architecture as he puts it. You have to see him, this little old man, the conviction and the ardor with which he talks about it all. He plans to leave everything to the city of Moscow. His son has a beautiful house in the grounds of the property and has already begun his own collection. Shchukin told me his father collected unusual eighteenth-century *objets de vitrine*—beautiful pieces for display in a glass case. But not everything is on display, and in the end, I couldn't help but imagine what it must have been like!

I visited the Shchukin Collection exhibition at the Louis Vuitton Foundation in 2017; it contained three hundred works from Shchukin's collection lent by the two Russian museums. As I walked through one of the galleries, filled with paintings by Matisse, which I thought had perhaps been hung to echo the room at Shchukin's mansion, I remembered Jules's remark about not yet being ready to appreciate them. I wondered if other paintings from Shchukin's collection might have been owned previously by Jules, or vice versa, and whether the two collectors had met again in Paris, after

Shchukin fled to France to escape the Russian revolution in 1918, and before his death in 1936.

The Shchukin exhibition evoked in me a deep feeling of sorrow that the Strauss collection had been broken up. If only something remained today of Jules's passion for art.

Had he hoped his collection would survive him? Did the premature death of his son, André, also an art lover and collector, bring to an end his dreams of passing things down to the next generation? I thought about Shchukin, who lost two sons and whose collection was confiscated and nationalized by Lenin in 1918. I thought about the great French collector Moïse de Camondo, who lost his two children in two world wars. Shchukin had wanted to leave his collection to the city of his birth. Camondo bequeathed his mansion and his art to the French state; everything inside the house remains, at his behest, exactly as it was in his lifetime—the living quarters, the dining room, with its menus and table plans for the dinners he once gave, are all open to the public today. In the upstairs gallery devoted to the family's story, the visitor learns about the successive tragedies that befell the family: in 1917 Moïse's beloved son, Nissim, a fighter in the French air force, went missing in action; in the early 1940s his daughter, Béatrice, her estranged husband, Léon Reinach, and their children, Fanny and Bertrand, were arrested by the Gestapo and deported. All four were murdered in Auschwitz. Yet inside 63 rue de Monceau, something of Moïse de Camondo and his family remains, so close.

No trace remains of my great-grandfather's collection,

only the imaginary museum that I am trying my best to piece together. I thought back to Jules's letter to Marie-Louise describing a display case filled with eighteenth-century objects that he had not seen but had imagined; like him, I dreamed of "what it must have been like."

I wanted to find out everything I could about Degas's little schoolboy, so I decided to journey back in time with him. The *Portrait of Jacques de Nittis as a Child* was bought at the 1932 auction by Jos Hessel. He then sold it to Simone Berriau, later to become the director of the Théâtre Antoine in Paris. Or did he buy the drawing on her behalf, on commission?

Hessel was a well-known art dealer and the director of the Bernheim-Jeune gallery until 1913. His wife, Lucy, modelled for Vuillard and became his mistress. Hessel was Vuillard's gallerist at the time. He went on to open his own gallery on rue de la Boétie. He had a reputation for being such a skilled negotiator that he was able to sell all sorts of things that his fellow dealers had failed to off-load.

Nadine's memory was a source of astonishment, but also occasionally of frustration. At times she would regale me with details that often seemed anecdotal, fragments of childhood memories. She recalled that the first ball my father was ever invited to was that of Lulu, Hessel's adopted daughter. She had no memory whatever of Hessel himself. She simply knew he was an "acquaintance" of her grandfather's.

"A friend? Did you ever see him at Avenue Foch?"

"Not a friend. Things were very different then, one didn't have many friends, just many acquaintances."

Nadine's responses were more significant than I realized. She gave me valuable insights into life at the time.

In 1936, Suzanne Berriau put the pastel up for auction at the main Parisian auction house, Hôtel Drouot. It was bought by André Schoeller, expert in nineteenth century French painting, president of the Art Editors Syndicate, and appraiser for Drouot. After the war Schoeller was accused of having sold artworks to the Nazis. Though he was eventually cleared of collaboration charges, he was fined for unjust enrichment. But in 1936, all this was yet to happen.

In 2014, the portrait was included in an exhibition at the Musée Marmottan in Paris, entitled "Impressionists at Home." In the catalog it's listed simply as having been lent from a "private collection." When I called the museum to find out the identity of the collector, the exhibition curator told me only that the owner wished to remain anonymous.

I was furious at being blocked in this way. But I wasn't prepared to give up, so I returned to the Musée d'Orsay to go through all the catalogs of Degas exhibitions in France and abroad from 1936 to the present day.

Helena gave me access to the room that holds exhibition catalogs from all over the world, going back to 1900, classified by date and by artist. I could help myself. There were dozens of catalogs in every language imaginable, and I painstakingly went through them all in the hope of finding some trace of the portrait of the little schoolboy and the name of its owner. I spent hours leafing through them. And then one day I came upon a photograph of a 1949 exhibition at the

Galerie Max Kaganovitch in Paris, showing the two works by Degas from Andrew's list, *The Start of the Race* and *Jacques de Nittis*. Both paintings had supposedly been sold by Jules in 1932, and both were declared stolen by the Nazis after the war by Marie-Louise.

Did the paintings belong to the gallerist, or had André Schoeller lent them for the exhibition?

I left a message for Andrew, asking him to call. He would certainly know how to find out. When he got back to me, he told me he was happy to help, but he didn't have a great deal of time, he was overwhelmed with work and away a lot on business. At this point in my investigation, I was so excited that I couldn't imagine there was anything in the world that could possibly be more important or interesting.

Andrew suggested I go to London to see his father, Michel, who was now retired and had "time on his hands." I thought I detected a slight hint of condescension, putting an end to my dream of Andrew and I working together as a team, he the expert, me his intrepid cousin, setting out together to find our forebear's vanished treasures.

VIII

"PLEASE CONTACT MICHEL STRAUSS"

Andrew's father, Michel, was only four years old in May 1940, when the Germans invaded France. His mother, Aline, was born into a wealthy Russian-Jewish banking family, who had come to France at the end of the nineteenth century. Aline's parents, Baron Pierre and Yvonne, changed the spelling of their surname in the 1920s, from de Gunzburg to de Gunzbourg. Theirs was a family of mavericks. Aline was a teenage champion golfer, while her brother, Philippe, finished second in the 1933 *24 Heures du Mans* motor race, and went on to join the British Special Operations Executive during the war. He was married to Antoinette, from whom Alexis later bought Jules's cosmetic containers. When Aline married André, the beloved son of Jules and Marie-Louise and also a knowledgeable collector, the union brought together two wealthy Jewish dynasties.

André died tragically young, of cancer, in 1939. In May 1940, the enterprising and independent-minded young widow escaped the German invasion at the wheel of an opentop Bentley, in which she and Michel drove to Biarritz, where she managed to obtain visas for them both to reach Lisbon and then New York. In 1943 she married the physicist Hans Halban, with whom she had two sons, Peter and Philippe. In 1946 the family moved to Oxford, where Halban had an appointment at the university. He and Aline divorced in 1955 and she went on to marry Riga-born philosopher and Oxford professor Isaiah Berlin.

After the war, Michel spent every holiday in France with his grandmother, Marie-Louise, who took him regularly to the Louvre and in so doing evidently transmitted to him *le goût Strauss*, the Strauss taste in art. I learned a lot about the family from Michel's 2011 memoir, *Pictures, Passions and Eye: A Life at Sotheby's*. At the 1949 auction, when the widowed Marie-Louise moved out of Avenue Foch into a smaller abode (she was able to return to the prewar apartment after 1945), Aline purchased some of the furniture and several eighteenth-century paintings for her thirteen-year-old son, in memory of his grandfather. Michel always regretted that he hadn't been allowed to attend the auction. I've always wondered if the memory of this missed opportunity was not at least in part the source of his vocation.

As though faithful to our illustrious forebear, Michel went on to have a brilliant career in the art world. He spent thirty years as head of the Impressionist and Modern Art department at Sotheby's, and it was he who came up with the innovation of allowing telephone bids at auction. While he only once actually wielded the auctioneer's hammer, Michel had seen, valued, and sold a huge number of Impressionist works of art. His son, Andrew, had taken up the torch, following him into the world of international auction houses. From André to Andrew, from Jules to Julia (the name of Michel's daughter), it was clear that Michel was devoted to his artistic heritage. Surely, if anyone did, he would know how to locate the missing paintings.

When we spoke on the phone, his gravelly voice and calm composure spurred me to contain my impatient excitement. He was pleasant without being warm, friendly without being demonstrative. I explained that I was doing research on a list of ten pictures that had apparently been sold in 1932 but went on to be declared stolen. I also told him what I'd discovered about the provenance of the *Portrait of Jacques de Nittis as a Child*.

He sent me a copy of an auction sale certificate, showing that André Schoeller had bought the pastel in 1936, at the auction of Simone Berriau's collection, on behalf of a certain Monsieur Schwenck. I asked him who Schwenck was, but Michel had no idea. I couldn't find any trace of him anywhere—there was no art collector or well-known figure of the time who bore that name.

The gap in its provenance had shrunk, but I still had no idea what had happened to the picture after the 1936 sale. Since it has had no identifiable owner since then, whenever the portrait is loaned out to museums it is always labeled as being "from a private collection."

Another theory occurred to me: perhaps Jules had bought it back at some point between 1936 and 1940. I returned to the Louvre to seek Helena's advice. I must have missed something. This would turn out to be one of the most interesting moments of my investigation, when I had not only to exhibit imagination and perseverance, but also to heed my intuition.

As I went through the catalogs one more time of every Degas exhibition held anywhere in the world since 1936, I considered various scenarios.

Perhaps Schwenck was a pseudonym made up by Jules so that he could discreetly purchase the pastel drawing through Schoeller, whom he knew because he had been the auctioneer for the 1932 Strauss sale four years earlier. But this was absurd. Jules was no Arsène Lupin, gentleman thief and master of disguise. And Schwenck is not an anagram of Strauss. I wondered briefly if perhaps he had purchased the pictures at the auction of his collection, using a false name—which would of course have been illegal; or if he had asked a friend to buy them on his behalf, planning to recover them as soon as he had the means. But there was no evidence for any of these hypotheses.

Nadine recalled having once met an American woman whose surname was Schwenk, a friend of her cousin Antoinette de Gunzbourg. She remembered nothing about her but her name. I googled, but found no mention of an American collector by that name. Even now, whenever I meet someone from the art world, I can't help asking if he or she has ever come across someone called Schwenck.

I spoke to Michel again. He listened and said little. It was the same thing every time: I'd get completely carried away telling him about my research, while he always remained curiously circumspect. I was afraid I was boring him with all my questions, that he must be irritated by my naive enthusiasm and my ignorance about art. Eventually, in a calm but decisive tone of voice, he interrupted my torrent of words: All that mattered, he said, were *hard facts*. I needed tangible, irrefutable evidence.

After I'd told him about my struggle to fill in the gaps in the picture's provenance, he sent me a document: In 2012 the New York-based gallery Mitchell-Innes & Nash had run a search through The Art Loss Register, a private body that investigates cases of stolen and looted art, on the provenance of the *Portrait of Jacques de Nittis as a Child*. Presumably the aim was to cleanse the work of all suspicion. Like anyone selling a piece of art, David Nash had to provide his clients with the complete provenance of the picture. The Art Loss Register had been able to prove that my family's claim was without basis. With this certificate of provenance, the picture could now be put up for sale.

Evidently there was nothing shady about the affair, and yet, I told Michel, I wasn't going to give up. Who had Nash purchased it from? Was there any way to find out? But Michel dug in his heels, and refused to question Nash, a former Sotheby's colleague. Even inquiring would be tantamount to an expression of suspicion. Michel told me to drop it. Of course, he had been operating in the art world for his entire career, and if nothing else my request certainly showed a lack of tact.

I had no idea how to proceed without Michel's help. I was stuck. Every painting goes on a kind of journey through time, with different owners at different periods. I was trying to follow all the different threads, but this time I was forced to give up.

Returning to the list of stolen pictures, I picked a Monet landscape to investigate and returned to the Musée d'Orsay.

Working my way through hundreds of haphazardly filed index cards, I was unable to lay my hands on the one for *Antibes, View from the Salis Gardens*. Monet had painted this view several times, and I found it rather dull, which led to me pulling up the wrong card several times as I muddled up the different versions.

As I was skimming the contents of a box labeled "Monet, landscapes, Antibes," I chanced upon an advertisement torn from a magazine for an auction held at Sotheby's in June 1980. I drew it out to look. I couldn't believe what I saw. In the middle of the page was a color reproduction of *Antibes, View from the Salis Gardens*. Beneath it, in bold type, the caption read, "Please contact Michel Strauss."

The sight of Michel's name made me feel deeply uneasy. What could have been going through his mind as he prepared the sale of a painting that had once belonged to his grandfather?

IX

COFFEE WITH AN EXPERT

Kneeling on the floor in the darkened living room of his London mews house, Michel shone an ultraviolet light onto a canvas, slowly and carefully illuminating every centimeter of the painting, from the little embroidered slippers that peeped out from underneath a long, paneled robe, to the young woman's deathly pale face and elaborately coiffed bright, coppery hair.

"Isn't she beautiful?"

I couldn't say I found her beautiful, with her neck swallowed up by an enormous ruff and her bulging eyes, but I had to admit there was something striking in the stiffness of her bearing. Not wanting to annoy Michel, who seemed to find an unexpected grace in her very lack of grace, I didn't reply.

A courier had brought over two life-size portraits, one a young man and one a young woman. "I don't know which to choose," he said.

"Look at this," he said, still on all fours, despite his age. "You can see where it's been restored."

He pointed to a long horizontal line on the dark background, invisible to the naked eye, but quite visible in the

55

ultraviolet light. He was still an expert, even though he was retired.

Officially I was in London for a conference at the British Library on looted art, but Henri had suggested that I make the most of my visit and pay a visit to my cousin. I was still in shock at my discovery that he had been involved in the sale of Jules's Monet, and I needed to see him rather than get lost in speculation.

I'd met Michel only once, but thirty years later I hadn't forgotten his distinctive face, with its strong features and deeply etched lines, his thick eyeglasses, and his still-dark hair. He invited me over at lunchtime, but there was nothing to eat. He offered me coffee. I was surprised to see there were no pictures on the walls. I supposed they must be hanging in his house in the country, where he lived with his new wife and several dogs.

He'd brought out several folders for me to look at. Inside, I found a jumble of papers, including an article about Jewish collectors before the war, the Strauss family tree going back five generations, and various photos of my father and Nadine with their cousins, Michel, Claude, and Jacques, when they were children.

There was also a black-and-white photo of Jules's study in Avenue Foch, which Michel thought must have been taken around 1920. It was the first time I had seen an image of the room. It was cluttered with antique furniture, shelves of books, and a large Aubusson tapestry. Two rows of Impressionist paintings hung on the damask-covered walls.

One portrait drew my attention. It was of a young girl with a rose fixed to her lustrous auburn hair, her hand lifted gracefully to her chin. *La Pensée* (*Portrait of a Girl in Thought*) was painted by Renoir in 1877 and bought by Jules in 1900. The painting seemed to light up the room. On either side of the stunning portrait hung two landscapes by Sisley that looked drab in comparison. I recognized them as two of the paintings on Andrew's list. A little higher up I saw Monet's *Les Pins Parasols, Cap d'Antibes* (*Stone Pines, Cap d'Antibes*), supposedly sold in 1932 but also later declared stolen. Lower down hung a Degas pastel, *Danseuse se coiffant* (*Dancer Arranging Her Hair*), the girl's profile turned toward a small, dark oil painting. Of course, Michel was familiar with all these works. He told me the name of each one. He must have seen them in museums or private homes, or at auction. He told me, laconically, as if it went without saying, that he had sold a few of them. I refused to contemplate the possibility that he was withholding information, but I didn't dare prod him further.

The photograph also showed several Regency chairs, each in a different style. In the foreground a small, plain table scattered with books gave the impression of studiousness amid the clutter. I imagined Jules admiring his pictures as he sat at his desk, getting up to rearrange them, or studying their provenance in *catalogues raisonnés*. I sensed a collector's passion for these Impressionist masterpieces, and could only imagine how sad he must have been at having to break up the collection in 1932. What had become of Monet's *Les Filets à Pourville* (*Fishing Nets at Pourville*), Degas's two young girls, Manet's sketch of a veiled woman? They had been sold to dealers, collectors, and museums, dispersed all over the world.

Together Michel and I discussed what we knew of the journey of each painting. I told him about my research at the Musée d'Orsay, that I hadn't yet uncovered anything out of the ordinary, and I still didn't understand how they could have been stolen by the Nazis.

I was both touched and reassured by Michel's willingness to share his memories with me. On the train on the way home, I opened his memoir. The inside flap of the book jacket showed the covers of the 1902 and 1932 auction catalogs. I read the chapter on his grandfather, whom he admired so much, in spite of having barely known him, having left France when he was a child: "When he died in 1943, he left neither land nor a significant portfolio of shares, but hundreds of works of art which had been put in storage at Tailleur's warehouse in Paris. They miraculously survived the war and were eventually recovered by my grandmother Mémé after the Liberation of Paris." Michel seemed to believe that the family had been incredibly lucky. But had it really been "miraculous"? Had his grandmother recovered the paintings after the Liberation? For the time being I had no evidence of anything, only the nagging question—how had a well-known Jewish collector been able to escape persecution in occupied Paris?

X

THE MIRACLE OF FORGETTING

The more I proceeded with my investigation, the more I realized how unlikely it was that Jules had been able to avoid his collection being seized by the Nazis. Every day I wrote to a different historian. My shelves were laden with books: *Si les tableaux pouvaient parler* (If Paintings Could Talk) by Corinne Bouchoux, *L'Art de la défaite* (The Art of Defeat) by Laurence Bertrand Dorléac, *L'Exode des musées* (The Exodus of the Museums) by Michel Rayssac. Even before the invasion of France, the Germans had drawn up a list of major French collections. They certainly would have known about Jules. Every Jewish collector figured on the list drawn up by the ERR, the *Einsatzstab Reichsleiter Rosenberg*, the special task force headed by the fanatical Nazi ideologue Alfred Rosenberg, who was tried at Nuremberg after the war and executed for war crimes. Beginning in July 1940, Rosenberg was responsible for the organized plunder of works of art belonging to Jewish collectors in occupied France. Around twenty-two thousand artworks were expropriated in the course of the war.

The headquarters of the ERR were established at the Jeu de Paume, where the looted artworks were stored before being sent to Germany. Rose Valland, an extraordinarily inspiring woman, was employed there as a curator before the war. She remained after the ERR took it over, pretending not to understand a word of German, all the while making detailed notes of the stolen works of art that were deposited there, compiling a detailed inventory, and recording what happened to each piece between 1940 and 1944. She wrote down the many visits Hermann Göring made to the museum to select which pieces to send to Germany. Her exceptional act of resistance made it possible after the war to recover a great number of these looted works of art. She was appointed a member of the Commission for the Recovery of Works of Art and made captain of the 1st French Army, and she worked with the Monuments Men, the corps of cultural experts appointed by the Allied forces to locate the stolen art and piece together the journey each work had taken.

The ERR was not the only body set up to seize works of art. In the summer of 1940, Otto Abetz, German ambassador to Paris, began a series of raids targeting the assets of well-known Jewish art dealers, collectors, and other wealthy Jews. This led to the creation of the *Möbel-Aktion,* or furniture operation, during which apartments left empty by their owners or tenants—after they had fled, been interned, or arrested during the "exodus" of June 1940 that followed the French capitulation to the German occupiers—were pillaged. There was also *La Carlingue,* the French Gestapo, set up in 1941 and known as the Bonny-Lafont gang, based at 93 rue Lauriston in Paris's 16th arrondissement. In 1942, an offshoot of the ERR, the Dienststelle Westen, initiated a large-scale operation to empty the apartments of thousands of Jews in and around Paris and throughout the whole of France, sort and ship them to the Reich. Was it one of these organizations that was responsible for the looting of Jules and Marie-Louise's paintings?

I called Thomas Weber, a friend of mine from Germany, whom I'd first met when I was a twenty-year-old student at Oxford and who was now a renowned historian specializing in the life of Hitler. He had recently unearthed some documents in South Africa that proved that Hitler himself had authored a 1923 book, *Adolf Hitler: His Life and Speeches*, long believed to have been penned by a German aristocrat. I was calling to congratulate him on his scoop, and to ask his help with solving the mystery of Andrew's list. The first thing he told me was that if the family had indeed petitioned for the return of their pictures, there would certainly be written evidence somewhere. He suggested looking in the *Bundesarchiv*, the German Federal Archives in Berlin, and put me in touch with one of his students, Marius Mazotti, who agreed to spend a day reviewing documents on my behalf.

A few days later I was holding a fat dossier in my hands. On the cover was written: "Élisabeth Strauss, Landesarchiv Berlin n° 1175/60." So this must have been where Andrew had found the list of pictures! It was one thing to have seen his scribbled list on a scrap of paper; it was quite another to find myself looking at six hundred pages of documents containing my grandmother's sixteen-year claims process against the German government, from 1958 to 1974. I went through the pages, which were mostly in German and in no particular order, with the assistance of Marius on the telephone, and Henri. The legal documents were mostly too complex to understand. But they helped me go back in time to imagine those years of my grandmother's life. I tried to establish a chronology.

In 1958, Élisabeth went to the Paris police headquarters, accompanied by two witnesses, Moïse V. and Monsieur P., to file a declaration of the theft of the ten paintings. Over the next decade and a half there were multiple written exchanges between French and German authorities, with much recourse to lawyers, antique experts, and art historians. I could only imagine my grandmother's increasing frustration at each stage of the fight.

I called Nadine to ask her if she remembered anything of this period. She was quite taken aback; no, her mother had never uttered a word to her about any claim. What about the witnesses—did she know them? She did remember Moïse; he was the concierge in the building on rue Lord-Byron to which her parents moved after the war, into the apartment she still lives in today. But she had never heard a word about any claim.

After several hours spent trying to decipher the files, we arrived at the stark verdict after sixteen years of legal proceedings: the German government declared that the family had provided insufficient evidence that the works had been stolen or sent to Germany. I was going to have to find evidence of both ownership and theft, of a forced transaction, or a wartime shipment to Germany. I felt quite crushed by the dossier's bulk and weight, both material and psychological.

How could Michel not have known, as he was preparing for the sale of Monet's *Antibes, View from the Salis Gardens*, that this very painting had been declared stolen by his own grandmother?

Who had got it wrong? My grandmother, who'd spent sixteen years in the pursuit of paintings which had in fact been sold in 1932? Or Michel, who writes in his memoir that "miraculously" everything had reappeared after the war?

I was deeply saddened by the Bundesarchiv documents, which bore witness to a lengthy legal battle that culminated in failure. No restitution, just a very small compensation for the only piece the Germans accepted had been stolen, a unique, six-inch-long, ancient Egyptian bronze lion. Alexis Kugel helped me establish its provenance prior to Jules's purchase of it in 1922 from Doctor Fouquet's famous Cairo collection.

"If ever it were to come on the market, I'd be the first to know," he assured me.

My grandmother Élisabeth would have been intimately acquainted with every detail of her father's collection. They had worked together researching Watteau, and she had been a member of the Society of the Friends of the Louvre her whole life. She must have known things about the collection that I was completely unaware of. I found it hard to believe she would have put in a claim for compensation without good reason. Thinking of her exhausting and ultimately fruitless fight for justice, I couldn't bear to think how sad and broken she must have been by the end of her life.

How was it possible that neither Nadine nor Michel had any recollection of the case? It's true that Michel was only twenty and living in London when his aunt Elisabeth put in her claim on behalf of the family; perhaps he simply wasn't told. But surely he would have made the connection when he was researching the provenance of the Monet? It's not in the interest of auction houses to draw attention to shady provenance; they have, historically, preferred to sell the works rather than get involved in returning them to their rightful owners. I considered the possibility that Michel had found himself pulled in two different directions, torn between responsibility to his family and professional duty, eventually deciding, bearing in mind the lack of "conclusive evidence," to go ahead with the sale.

I have read about people rejecting the idea that they had been victims of spoliation, perhaps as the psychoanalysts Jean Laplanche and Jean-Bernard Pontalis wrote (referring to Freud) of "a defense mechanism consisting of a refusal by the subject to recognize the reality of a traumatizing perception." It's a way of forgetting, or "putting aside" painful memories. Was it possible that we, Jules's descendants, were suffering from this? Strauss means ostrich in German—had we actively decided to put our heads in the sand to avoid the truth? If it is indeed possible to choose to forget, history is nothing if not a little cruel: Michel would have had to forget in order to sell the painting.

I decided to phone him and ask him directly if he had any recollection of Elisabeth's claim.

"It was a very long time ago," was all he said.

I could have pressed the point, but there was something sad and stubborn in his voice that made me drop the subject.

Meanwhile, I began to notice that whenever I mentioned the name of someone involved in the claim Nadine, who had been insisting for months that she knew nothing about anything, would summon up a precise and specific memory.

"Does the name Paul Feher mean anything to you?"

"It certainly does. He was that terrible lawyer who cost us a fortune! Your grandmother went to a great deal of trouble, you know."

Nadine had never spoken to me about thefts or claims. Yet all of a sudden, here she was talking about all the "trouble" her mother had gone to. Aware that these little bursts of memory might not last, I tried to push her a little more.

"Do you know what really happened? Why did she decide to put in a claim for pictures that had been sold twenty-five years earlier? What made her think they'd been stolen?"

"Oh, she must have been mistaken."

Her eyes grew misty and unfocused. I didn't want to stir up any more upsetting memories. But I couldn't help wondering how a person could be "mistaken" for sixteen years.

XI

AN EXPRESSION

Nadine entrusted me with a black-and-white photograph of Jules. For months it sat propped up on the mantelpiece in my bedroom. The old man's distant expression made me think of Verlaine's description of "beautiful eyes concealed by veils." I have no idea when it was taken. Jules is an elderly man in the photograph, elegant and well-groomed, but a touch lost in his loose-fitting suit. His face is long and gaunt, and his gray hair swept back. His small, round, metal spectacles—are these the veils of sadness?—give him a somber air. He isn't looking at the camera, or even to one side. His gaze is somewhere else altogether.

Perhaps he is thinking about André. "The loss of our beloved son, who shared so many of our interests, has left an immense void; we must bow to it," he wrote to Germain Bazin, head curator of the Louvre's Department of Painting, a month after André's death. Nadine had found the letter tucked away inside a file on her bookshelf. She gave me another letter, dated November 1939 and sent by Jules from the Château de Brécourt to his nephew Erwin, in America. André had purchased the château a few years earlier, and the whole Strauss family took refuge there for a period after war was declared. "Alas, everything reminds me of him, his face never leaves me. It is the most terrible tragedy! And yet somehow I must carry on."

Had the photograph Nadine had given me been taken at the beginning of the war? Jules looks lost in thought, dignified, and terribly sad.

I concentrated on his face as if I were trying to lose myself in him. Where was the insatiable collector, the indefatigable walker who strode through the streets of Paris in search of unusual and beautiful things? Where was the passionate aesthete, who liked nothing better than to pick out beautiful vermeil centerpieces for the table and bouquets of flowers when their friends and fellow collectors, the Wormsers, came for dinner? Had he been the lover of Olga, André Wormser's wife?

Who were you, Jules?

I organized a session for my writing students in which we focused on the portrait, to see if they could coax something out of it. But although I kept hoping for an epiphany, the moment when the scraps of information I had gleaned about my grandfather would finally come together and reveal something of who he really was, my sense of him remained stubbornly indistinct. I tried to talk to Nadine again.

"Tell me everything you know about Jules."

"Well," she said. "He was born in Frankfurt in 1861. His father was a banker who died of tuberculosis when he was quite young. I believe he had five brothers and sisters, but I never met any of them. He came to Paris on his own in 1881 and found a job as a foreign exchange broker, but he gave that up after the First World War to focus on art. He had a strong German accent—not that I noticed! He had an eye for a pretty woman. He was very amusing. He loved to spoil me; he used to take me to PamPam to eat caviar after school. Whenever he picked me up from school he never crossed at the crossing, which always drew furious glances from the policeman."

I thought of a drawing by Sempé of an elegant monsieur in a suit and a Homburg hat, crossing the street hand in hand with a little pirouetting girl.

"And he smoked two packets of Gitanes a day."

He didn't tell his wife everything. Nadine suspected that he hid his purchases from his wife, leaving some of the pictures he bought with the dealers. This was another path to be explored. Unfortunately my aunt didn't know the dealers' names, which would make it a lengthy task to locate their descendants. Most were Jewish, and their art had been expropriated in different ways. Paul Rosenberg managed to flee, but the vault where he had left his collection for safekeeping was discovered by the Nazis and everything was taken. In some cases, a provisional administrator had been appointed to liquidate the stock, as was the case for the Bernheim-Jeune gallery, an early promoter of the work of Cézanne, Bonnard, and Seurat, among many others. The personal possessions of the two Bernheim brothers, Josse and Gaston, were also seized by the ERR.

At Helena's prompting, I began to compile a psychological profile of my great-grandfather. Perhaps I had inherited some of his character traits. Could I detect a tiny bit of Jules in me? But no. Still he eluded me.

In the photograph he looks pensive, austere, a little guarded. Suddenly it's not Jules I see but my father, wearing his familiar preoccupied expression. They both had the same low, narrow moustache that grew slightly over the top lip, the same faintly absent air. My father never used to talk to me about his worries, or reminisce in my presence. By the end of his life, he was too ill to speak, and I often caught him looking at me with an anxious, lost expression. He was distant, I didn't know where his thoughts might be taking him. I recalled the poem by Jean Pellerin he had chosen as the epigraph for his Masters dissertation on Proust:

> *Hold on to this moment,*
> *Before it rushes away*
> *Time slips, hives off*
> *Why is that the thing we love*
> *Is always already in the past?*

After he and his family escaped to the Free Zone in 1940, he enrolled at the university in Aix-en-Provence to finish his literature studies, which had been interrupted by the Vichy anti-Jewish laws that prevented him from taking the oral exam for entry to the prestigious École Normale Supérieure. A few months later he joined the Free French Forces. He was only nineteen, and yet he must already have been familiar with a feeling of nostalgia. That whole Parisian world he had left was now lost forever. Did he have a premonition that he would never see his grandfather again?

I knew full well I'd never truly know Jules, that however hard I studied the photograph of his face, I would never uncover all his secrets. But now, after I had spent so many hours in his company, something seemed to light up in his eyes, and I could swear he was looking at me. Steady and dignified, his expression gave me the strength I needed to carry on.

XII

TROY

When I was twelve, I went through a phase of reading and rereading a children's book about the incredible discoveries of Heinrich Schliemann, the nineteenth century businessman-turned-archeologist who set out to locate the city of Troy, using Homer as his guide. After a lengthy search, he uncovered evidence of seven cities, each built upon a previous one. During the excavations he dug so deeply that he destroyed one of the historical layers of the city of Troy.

I fantasized that one day I, too, would find a mystery to solve, a secret to decipher, a treasure trove to uncover. Was Jules's collection my Troy, my Priam's treasure? I was still in the early stages of my excavations, and I wasn't even sure what I was looking for or what I might find. But it was exciting to be sifting through my family's past. It was also impossible not to wonder about the contemporary value of the pictures in the Strauss collection. Tens of millions of dollars, without a doubt. Almost obsessively, I was trying to retrace the journey of each picture on Andrew's list, from the day it had first caught Jules's eye and he decided to buy it, right up to the day my grandmother declared it stolen by the Nazis. A whole itinerary to be pieced together.

Helena suggested I visit the Louvre documentation center, whose entrance in the Tuileries was flanked by two bronze lions. Just as at the Musée d'Orsay, all I had to do to be granted access to this secret place, known only to researchers, art historians, and fellow detectives of the past, was show proof of my identity.

None of the archives here are digitalized. Kilometers of shelving line the walls from floor to ceiling, each laden with dusty cardboard boxes with handwritten labels, classified according to century and artist, some so high up that I had to climb a swaying wooden stepladder to consult them. Just a few other people were there, including an elderly man muttering to himself as he went through boxes filing pages of old art magazines. It was hard to believe I was inside the world's largest museum.

The grumpy old gentleman turned out to be a retired curator who still came to the museum every day. He seemed to consider it his private sanctum, and was furious when I sat down at his table. He sniped and grumbled as he cut out articles and slipped them into folders. What on earth was he up to in the bowels of the Louvre?

I was shown a shelf of archives on collectors and dealers. My heart thudding in my chest, I opened a box labeled "Strauss," and took out a dossier on Jules containing cuttings about the 1902 and 1932 sales. And then I discovered a folder entitled "Jules Strauss: Patron," from which I drew out an article:

Jules Strauss
Frankfurt 1861–Paris 1943

Jules Strauss was an avid collector of furniture, *objets d'art*, and paintings both classical and modern. His first collection, of seventy-one Impressionist paintings, including almost the complete works of Sisley, such that it earned him the sobriquet Monsieur Sisley, was broken up at a 1902 auction in Paris (Drouot, 3rd May). The second, which comprised eighty-five Impressionist paintings by a broader range of artists, was in turn sold off in 1932 (Galerie G. Petit, 15th Dec.). His furniture was dispersed at two posthumous sales, the first in 1949 (Galerie Charpentier, 27th May) and the second in 1961 (Palais Galliera, 7th March; preface J. Dupont).

Between 1921 and 1928 Strauss donated four paintings to the Louvre, *Paysage avec architectures* (*Landscape with Architecture*) by Lajoue, *La Retraite de Russie* (*The Retreat from Russia*) by Raffet, a painting by Colson, and a drawing and a sculpture, *Saint Sebastien* by Pompe. He also instigated the Louvre's new framing policy in 1900, when he began seeking out antique frames to replace the Empire-style frames that dominated at the time. He donated some sixty frames that today showcase some of the museum's most famous masterpieces from all different periods.

> *Donors to the Louvre*, Paris (RMN), 1989, index of donors, p. 328.

"Dispersed" was the word that struck me. Nothing remains of his collections. I had no idea that Jules had donated anything to the Louvre in the 1920s. According to the Louvre website: on 6 June 1921 a painting by Raffet, *La Retraite en Russie* (*The Retreat from Russia*). In 1924, an architectural drawing by Lajoue. In 1927, a sixteenth-century panel by Siesseneger, *Les Enfants de Maximilien* (*The Children of Maximilien*). In March 1928, an early eighteenth-century *Portrait d'un homme* (*Portrait of a Man*) by Jean-François Colson.

I stared at images of these paintings on my computer screen, unable to appreciate their charms. I was disappointed to discover that not one of them is on display. Along with hundreds of others, they are held in the museum's reserves. I wasn't going to be able to see them.

This was also the first time I had come across any mention of Jules's gift of frames to the Louvre. As I went through a file containing the original correspondence between the curators and my great-grandfather, I came across a cache of letters. Their tone was both cordial and courteous. One, dated 1935, was addressed to a curator, Jacques Dupont, later to become Inspector General of Historic Monuments—and the person who had written the preface to the catalog for the 1961 auction:

Monsieur,

Quite by chance I recently came across a splendid Renaissance frame measuring 84 cm by 61 cm, with reverse molding and open-work carving. The dimensions almost exactly match those of Raphael's *Balthazar Castiglione*, which is currently displayed in an Empire frame (which truth be told rather suits it, though it is a little modest for Raphael's most stunning portrait). I would like to donate the frame to the Louvre—after, of course, we have checked that it is suitable.

If you approve, let us fix a date to meet at the Petit Palais to see it *in situ*.

Yours most sincerely,
Jules Strauss

I was intrigued, curious to find out more about these frames. I knocked at the door to the office of one of the curators, which happened to be right next to the documentation center. I was surprised to learn that the newly appointed head of the collection of frames at the Louvre knew nothing of the Jules Strauss donation either. All she could show me was a 1961 article in the magazine *Connaissance des Arts*, in which the journalist Hélène Demoriane writes that it was Jules Strauss who was behind the new taste at the Louvre for high-quality, specially selected frames corresponding to the period of the painting. He had the idea after coming across a fourteenth century Florentine frame at the gallery of the well-known antique frame dealer Lebrun. He had it delivered to the Louvre so that it could be tried out on Leonardo da Vinci's *Virgin of the Rocks,* to replace the painting's Empire frame. Subsequently, he purchased another frame from the same period for Leonardo's *Portrait of an Unknown Woman* and, as mentioned in his letter to Jacques Dupont, for Raphael's *Portrait of Baldassare Castiglione.* I felt a certain pride at the thought that my forebear's taste had had such an influence on one of the greatest museums in the world; what seems quite normal and obvious today had not so long ago been a pioneering concept.

In another box labeled "Jules Strauss: Collector," I found more letters addressed to Jules, the last dated 1939, in which the then curator, Germain Bazin, thanks Jules and Marie-Louise for their gift, after my great-grandfather was given the go-ahead to purchase frames for sixty paintings. After the war Bazin would go on to extend the initiative, orchestrating a major framing program at the museum. The final missive, a moving letter of condolence to Marie-Louise dated October 1943, not long after Jules's death, I found particularly moving, for the way Bazin lauds the intent behind Jules's generosity:

"While some connoisseurs wish their names to be publicly associated with their largesse, Monsieur Jules Strauss, with affecting modesty, preferred to manifest his generosity with gifts of a more discreet nature, that were no less appreciated by us. Several of the greatest masterpieces in the Louvre owe to him their magnificent antique frames. I will never forget the hours I was fortunate to spend with him when he came to the museum to view our collection of antique frames, to which he had made such a significant contribution."

If only my father had taken me to the museum and shown me the paintings his grandfather had donated. How I wish we could have stood in front of *The Retreat from Russia*, wondering what it was that had drawn Jules to it, why he had chosen this subject, what had inspired him to donate this painting rather than another to the Louvre. How I would have loved to have walked with him through the grand gallery of the Italian Renaissance, admiring paintings by Raphael, Veronese, and Leonardo da Vinci, listening to tales of Jules and his hunt for their frames. We would have retraced his steps through the museum, where he seems to have felt quite at home. He liked to visit on Tuesdays, when it was closed to the public, to try out frames on different paintings.

Yet my father had never breathed a word about Jules's donations. As if time had erased it all—the memories of beautiful things and terrible tragedies alike.

The Lebrun frame emporium is still in existence. I sent an email, and within a few hours received a response from the director that went far beyond what I'd hoped.

Madame,

I am indeed aware that we sold a number of frames to Monsieur Strauss. I believe he was a friend of my grandfather, Jacques Lebrun. I still have in my possession an armchair, which I'm extremely fond of, that my grandfather bought from your great-grandfather.

Unfortunately, the gallery is closed for the summer, so may I suggest that we arrange to meet at the beginning of September?

I hoped I'd be able to see this armchair. I wanted to see and touch everything that had once belonged to Jules. I was so thrilled to think of the two friends with their shared passion, hunting down Renaissance frames that would fit the paintings in the Louvre.

It was as if eighty years had just been swept away.

Back in the archive, I dug up an article by none other than the former curator, the old gentlemen who was always muttering to himself as he rummaged through his dusty boxes. In an essay entitled "A Critical Study of Framing," published in the *Revue de l'Art* in 1987, he writes,

In 1935, an enthusiastic amateur collector took it upon himself to frame, at his own expense—thanks to, shall we say, his 'Cousin Pons' discoveries—some of the best-known paintings in the Louvre (including, for example, Mantegna's *Madonna of Victory)*, assisted by a young curator in the Department of Painting and future Inspector General of Monuments, Jacques Dupont. Another member of the department,

the future head curator Germain Bazin, got wind of
what had begun as a personal project, and went on
to undertake in 1945 the most spectacular reframing
venture ever undertaken in the modern era.

The curator's remarks seemed unexpectedly grudging. What
did he mean by Cousin Pons? Why did I get the sense he
was minimizing Jules's generosity? I picked up Balzac's novel,
which I have no doubt Jules had read, and discovered, in
the eponymous figure of Cousin Pons, an erudite man of a
long-distant era who was able to spot rare pieces and ferret
out treasures other people missed.

In the few lines of the article, I detected for the first time
a tone of contempt, a sort of aversion to, and perhaps even
jealousy of, an elderly Jewish collector who had both the lei-
sure and the means to make "discoveries."

XIII

JULES'S CHAIR

Lebrun Frames has been housed since the 1930s at the same address, on rue du Faubourg-Saint-Honoré, barely a hundred meters from Nadine's apartment. In recent years, the building has been entirely renovated; the gallery on the ground floor is the only thing that hasn't changed. Lebrun's granddaughter Virginie welcomed me into a room at the back of the establishment, where dozens of frames of every size and style hung on the walls or leaned against one another on the floor: a jumble of beautiful things, of gilt and dust. It took me a few minutes to make out a few other beautiful objects: a Louis XV table with a marble pedestal, a Rococo cheval dressing mirror.

And then, in the center of the room, Jules's carved wooden chair, with its torn and threadbare red-and-white embroidered silk upholstery. I asked Virginie what period it was, for I had never seen such elaborately carved wooden legs before; she told me it was a Louis XIV piece.

Bending down to examine the legs, I saw they were riddled with woodworm. They looked as if they might crumble into dust at any moment. It was sad to see this shabby chair in the middle of the dimly lit room, looking worn and abandoned. Yet Virginie assured me that she was very attached to it, that this was the chair she sat in every day to work and receive clients. I felt a twinge of irritation that she didn't take more care of it.

She took down from the wall a narrow, rectangular, Louis XIII mirror, its frame draped in cobwebs. It had hung there since she was a child.

On the back was a thumbtacked piece of paper: "Two mirrors are marked inside. PV Quesbec. ME (see Lami, *Dictionary of 18th-Century French Furniture*). Also, written in pencil at the time 'made by Lenfant the elder, rue St Denis St François, Paris 1753, this 19th of June.'"

"Jules Strauss wrote that," she said.

I found myself looking for the first time at the elongated upstrokes of my great-grandfather's handwriting. More than seventy years earlier he had jotted down the provenance of these mirrors on a piece of paper that he had then pinned to the back.

Virginie explained that Monsieur Lebrun had bought them from Jules before the war. "They became good friends," she told me. When they met, in the early 1930s, her grandfather was in his thirties, while Jules was already approaching seventy. And so it was that the granddaughter of a frame dealer owned more mementoes of my great-grandfather than I did.

I was burning with desire to buy them, I wanted so badly to get them back, but how could I possibly ask this woman who had kindly invited me in and shown me all she owned? I barely knew her.

She brought out some documents to show me. One was an order book from the 1960s for repairs to picture frames. Among the clients listed were Marie-Louise Strauss, rue Mirabeau, and Élisabeth Baer, rue Lord-Byron.

I took some photographs, then sat down in Jules's chair, where I stayed until the end of our meeting. Virginie perched opposite me on an uncomfortable-looking stool. I should have offered her the chair, but I didn't move. I had the urge to sit there forever.

"If you ever decide to sell this chair or the mirrors, please let me know," I said.

"You know, the Strauss collection is legendary here," she replied.

Her answer made me smile. Had she not the slightest inkling what the chair might mean to me?

I told her the family owned nothing that had belonged to Jules apart from a few worthless mementoes and a fake Renoir. I suppose I was trying to make her feel a bit sorry for me, so she might consider selling the pieces, or maybe even give them to me in homage to Jules. I felt slightly ashamed of being so manipulative, but I couldn't help finding the story of my family so cruel and unjust: surely these last remaining objects ought to be returned to us?

Virginie rummaged through some papers as I told her about Jules's apartment and showed her the photograph of his study. The chair wasn't in the picture. I would have to go through all the pictures of Avenue Foch taken in the 1920s.

There were some other documents in the Lebrun archives from 1961, records filled in by employees when a client brought a frame in to be repaired, with notes about the piece in question. I wondered whether there might be similar documents from earlier in the century.

Virginie opened a large accounts ledger that began in 1935 and went up to 1943. I saw several familiar names: the Gimpels, the Rosenbergs, the Javals, names I had come across at the archives of the Foreign Ministry and elsewhere, families whose collections had been stolen by the Nazis. "Monsieur Strauss"—could this be Jules? The name cropped up four times between 1935 and 1942.

1942: "Monsieur Strauss 1 C Dutch stripped and stained pearwood color Michel 15—Dramet 64."

Michel was the name of the employee who did fifteen hours of work. Dramet had worked on it for sixty-four hours.

In order to confirm this was Jules, I would need to see a document with his address. I hoped Madame Lebrun would have the time and the inclination to go through the archives in the basement.

I was a little hesitant to broach the subject of what had happened to the frame emporium during the war, until she mentioned that the family house outside Paris had been bombed.

"I don't know, oddly enough. It closed, I suppose."

Then she opened an account ledger from the years 1935 to 1940.

"Actually, it seems like they worked right through the war," she said with some surprise.

Over seventy years later, even though she worked in the family business, she had apparently never asked herself the question. Privately, I wondered if they ought to have shut up shop—if the very fact of continuing to work during the Occupation made them by definition culpable.

I explained that any documents regarding the restoration of frames during that period held in the company's archive might help me to identify the paintings that were in Jules's possession just before the war, and to get a better sense of what the Nazis might have looted. She didn't flinch when I said the word "looted." Emboldened by the historical relationship between our families, I told her about my project. She listened, astonished, and promised me that if she found any such documents, she would certainly let me know. She hadn't realized how precious such archives are for people trying to establish provenance.

Before I left, she showed me a page on the company's website:

Jules Strauss was another of the gallery's regular clients. He was an important donor of antique frames to the Louvre, including that of Leonardo da Vinci's *Virgin of the Rocks*, which came from the Lebrun collection.

Virginie told me that the frame had needed to be shaved very finely fifty times to make it fit the painting.

When I showed Henri a photograph of the chair, he was convinced he had seen it somewhere before. A few hours later he sent me a 1961 article from *Connaissance des Arts*:

"Jules Strauss had a passion for unusual pieces and owned a stunning collection of Regency-era furniture, each piece distinguished by a few unexpected and atypical details in either form or decoration. [. . .]

"This carved wooden chair is typical of Strauss's taste in seating. As a keen and knowledgeable collector of 'curiosities,' he was attracted by the bold contours of the curved legs, the latticed seat, the decorative carvings of shells and scrolls of acanthus, and the unusual shape of the backrest, a kind of truncated version of the Louis XIV style."

These were the kinds of detail that I would imagine few people care about anymore: the shape of a chair's legs, whether it was a Louis XIV or Regency piece. If even Monsieur Lebrun's granddaughter, who sat on this chair every day, paid little heed to it, what traces remained of Strauss's taste?

Indeed, "what remains of Jules Strauss?" appeared a few lines on in the article. "He wrote nothing, passed down nothing apart from a few brief notes intended as commentary on paintings lent out to innumerable exhibitions. The donations he made to the Louvre and the Musée Carnavalet are, for the uninformed, lost in obscurity in the bowels of the museums. As for his fabulous collections—fabulous in terms of size and breadth—they exist no longer except in the pages of four auction catalogs. Two words sum up what one might call 'the Jules Strauss phenomenon': Gift and faith."

XIV

BEGINNER'S LUCK

Memory is a strange thing. Nadine's tended to be hit-and-miss, and was often preceded by deep absorption. Together we would travel back to her childhood, down some unexpected path—a patisserie that no longer existed, a 1930s movie actress, summer holidays in Saint-Briac. I was trying to throw light on dimly remembered episodes, to delve into blanked-out chapters of family history. It was easier to talk to her face-to-face than over the telephone, so I would visit her at home, sometimes for just an hour or two. I would bring her little treats: coffee ice cream or English biscuits. She was no longer surprised by my line of questioning.

"Nadine, do you have any idea why Jules and Marie-Louise moved out of Avenue Foch during the war?"

"Because it was too big, I suppose," she said. "They rented it from the Phoenix insurance company. Did you know that in 1900 Jules took over the apartment from Georges Feydeau?"

I had heard this story before, but this time I was struck by the clash of such different worlds, boulevard theatre and people being forced from their homes during the Occupation.

"Where did they go?" I asked.

"They moved to 54 Avenue d'Iéna, the building owned by the parents of Michel's mother, the Gunzbourgs."

"Do you recall them moving? When was this exactly?"

"I wasn't in Paris, remember! We were already in Aix-en-Provence, your father was at university there and I was in high school. I never saw Jules again."

Nadine told me about their life in Aix, all the fun she had, how she hated school, her pretty friend Mireille, my father working on his dissertation about Proust. I'd heard these stories dozens of times, only half listening, but now it was as though I was hearing them for the first time, each distinct element becoming an important clue in my quest.

It took me a long time to pick up the telephone to call Claude Sorbac, my father's first cousin, born the year before he was. I felt the trepidation of a child who is afraid she might hear unpleasant things about other members of the family. For some reason, as he grew older, my father had grown apart from Claude and his brother, Jacques, and we almost never saw them. I have a vague memory of arguments during my childhood. But eventually I decided I had to speak to Claude, who had moved to Buenos Aires after the war, hoping he might remember something. It wasn't an easy conversation. He was hard of hearing and, like Nadine, he had a tendency to go off on a tangent. But I learned one thing.

"I was the only person from my generation of the family who saw Jules in Paris during the war," he told me. "In

1943 I managed to cross the demarcation line to visit him on his sickbed."

"Where?"

"Rue du Ranelagh."

"Rue du Ranelagh? Not Avenue d'Iéna?" I was confused.

"No, he was living at my parents'. He died in July."

This was how I discovered that Jules and Marie-Louise had moved not once but twice; in 1941 they moved in with their daughter Françoise, now back Paris and living in a different neighborhood. Later I asked Nadine if this was just before or just after their son-in-law Roger, Françoise's husband and Claude's father, was arrested and deported. She wasn't sure—she reminded me again she wasn't in the city at the time. I tried to talk to Claude about his father, but he couldn't hear me properly and kept changing the subject. He was much more forthcoming about Jules's taste for Impressionist art, "paintings of happiness," and the world of Jules's family, "well-born" Jews from Frankfurt, than about his father's arrest.

It was easier to talk to the Sorbac cousins of my own generation. The shift to the next generation seemed to have dulled the tragedy. Marie-Hélène, Jacques's daughter, shared my interest in our family history, and we began speaking regularly. She told me that on the day of his arrest Roger had just given a hiding to Jacques, his younger son, when he opened the front door to the police. Jacques was still furious with his father, and this haunted him for the rest of his life. A little later he and his brother, Claude, joined the Free French

Forces; Jacques, at only seventeen, was one of the youngest French commandos.

Had Jules and Marie-Louise witnessed their son-in-law's arrest? How had they managed to remain living at an address known to the Gestapo, with the ever-present risk that they in turn might be arrested?

Helena suggested that I make a chronological chart retracing these events, using the various documents and pieces of information I had gathered. But the assignment turned out to be unexpectedly complex, because none of the dates coincided. All the different elements kept shifting and I kept having to begin again. It was clear that each auction corresponded to some significant change in the family's circumstances. The 1932 sale was linked to the stock market crash and subsequent financial ruin of Jules's brothers-in-law. The 1949 sale coincided with Marie-Louise moving out of the grand apartment on Avenue Foch, which necessitated getting rid of furniture and paintings. The 1961 sale of the Strauss estate took place soon after Marie-Louise's death.

Each new element had to be inserted into the chronology: a letter from Jules to Nadine sent to her at the Château de Brécourt in August 1940; a copy of my father's dissertation, dated May 1941, addressed to his grandmother at 54 Avenue d'Iéna; Claude's visit in June 1943 to see his grandfather, now living with Françoise on rue du Ranelagh, and so on.

I sketched out a sort of map retracing Jules and Marie-Louise's life in wartime. I must have started all over again ten times at least, correcting details each time I discovered something new. It was very approximate, with a lot of gaps and question marks, and I grew increasingly frustrated at my slow progress, feeling as though I was wasting time on minutiae. I was desperate to work out whether and how the story of the Strausses became intertwined with the story of looted art.

At the National Archives in Pierrefitte, north of Paris, I looked through various dossiers of Aryanization, searching according to family name and address. I didn't find anything, probably because Jules had stopped working as a banker long before the war. Where and how should I look next? I contacted Marc Masurovsky and gave him a brief summary of the family history. He replied,

"Fifty-four Avenue d'Iéna, the building belonging to the Gunzbourgs (Aline's parents) was occupied by Alfred Rosenberg's organization the ERR, the service responsible for the expropriation of large Jewish art collections."

I couldn't believe it. Had Jules and Marie-Louise rushed headlong into a trap when they moved into the building?

I wasn't interested in spending hours researching the ERR, I just wanted to know if the Strausses had been among the families whose art collections were confiscated by Rosenberg's task force and stored in the Jeu de Paume before being sent to Germany.

All the details are available online; it took no time to ascertain that the Strauss collection had not been among those seized by the Rosenberg task force. The mystery remained.

I went over what I had found out so far.

In 1940, Jules and Marie-Louise Strauss left Avenue Foch for unknown reasons. They moved to 54 Avenue d'Iéna into their son André's old apartment. A few months later the ERR requisitioned the building, where in 1942 Alfred Rosenberg set up the offices of the *Dienststelle Westen*, which had taken over the running of the *Möbel-Aktion*, under the direction of Kurt von Behr. I wasn't clear on all the dates. If the Strausses had crossed paths with Colonel von Behr, it surely would have been impossible for them to escape. At some point in 1941, Jules and Marie-Louise left Avenue d'Iéna and moved in with their daughter Françoise and her family on rue du Ranelagh, where Jules died in July 1943.

What did Jules and Marie-Louise do with their furniture and art each time they moved? And how had their collection escaped the Nazis' grasp?

I called my historian friend Thomas Weber again to find out more about the spoliations. I wanted to know how the *Möbel-Aktion* functioned.

"The Germans cleared out apartments belonging to Jews, left empty after the people who lived there were deported," he told me. "They took everything. Furniture, works of art, everything."

"Jules wasn't deported," I said, "but it's possible his apartment was emptied. Do you know how I can get hold of a list of stolen effects?"

"Apparently all the lists were burned. But why don't you

call Carolin Lange, a former student of mine? She researches provenance for a Munich museum. She might be able to help."

This was the first time I'd come across the job of researching the provenance of looted works of art. I wrote to Carolin Lange with a few details about my family's history, including the fact that Jules had moved house twice to escape the clutches of the Nazis. That same evening, she emailed me a link to the website of the French Ministry of Culture.

On my computer screen, the black-and-white drawing looked drab and dull, but what was written alongside was to occupy my mind for an entire year, to the point of obsession; it would take me from the Parisian suburb of La Courneuve to Dresden, via a reader's desk at the Ministry of Culture. The label next to the drawing read:

MNR

A Shepherd

Attributed to Giovanni Battista Tiepolo

Description:

The drawing, numbered 127, was sold at auction at the Hotel Drouot on 15th November 1928 for 5200 francs, to Monsieur Strauss.

On 22nd May 1943 it was acquired for the Linz Museum by Ehrard Göpel, through the intermediary Victor Mandl, 9 rue Boccador, Paris; shortly before the end of the war it was taken to Alt Aussee where it was stored with the rest of the Linz Landesmuseum collection, and registered under the number 9082.

In 21st January 1948 it was returned to France on the 24th convoy bound from Munich. On 26th October 1950 it was placed in the Department of Prints and Drawings before being formally assigned to the National Museums of France and allocated to the Department of Prints and Drawings at the Louvre.

If this Monsieur Strauss was indeed my great-grandfather, who were all the other people through whose hands the drawing had passed during the different stages of its journey back to Paris? And why had the Louvre at no point over the last seventy years attempted to contact Monsieur Strauss's descendants?

XV

A SHEPHERD, SEEN FROM BEHIND

February 2017. After months of research, I put in a claim for the drawing's return to the offices of the MNR, the Musées Nationaux Récupérations (National Museums Artwork Recovery Division). The Tiepolo drawing was one of two thousand artworks that were recovered in Germany after the war and are still held by various French national museums pending their return to their owners.

I obtained permission to see the Tiepolo at the Louvre's Department of Prints and Drawings. Among its holdings, the department keeps in storage drawings, engravings, and prints too fragile to be on permanent exhibition. Though I was allowed to view the drawing, I obviously had no idea if doing so would lead to its return. I had the right to see it now, but no idea if I would ever see it again.

Michel came over from London for the occasion. We arranged to meet in the Tuileries Gardens, by the two bronze lions that give their name to this entrance to the museum. It was raining. Michel stood waiting for me on the damp gravel, a tall, slightly stooped figure. I greeted him warmly, though I found him a little intimidating and detached. He hardly smiled, and appeared unwilling to waste his breath on superfluous conversation.

Once inside, I followed him down the long corridors of the museum. In spite of his age and the fact that he walked with a cane, he was imposing. When we reached the Department of Prints and Drawings, we both immediately noticed the name Jules Strauss carved twice onto the marble panel of benefactors' names. He had donated drawings in 1925 and 1928. I took a photograph of this unusual moment: the eighty-year-old grandson standing alongside the name of his illustrious grandfather.

A Shepherd, the Tiepolo drawing I had been researching for over a year, had been brought out for us and placed on a small stand in the center of the room. We followed the head of the department across the magnificent room, with walls covered in gilded wooden paneling and windows looking onto the Tuileries. The room was so vast that I barely noticed the few scattered tables, supported by marble columns, at which researchers worked. Against such a lavish background, the humble little drawing on its stand looked lost.

The curator stood by as we contemplated it. "Take your time," she told us.

In my head it was as if I heard two voices arguing. One wanted to celebrate the thrilling implications of this event, while the other insisted on playing it down, pointing out that the drawing was small, rather yellowed, and completely drowned in this opulent space.

But how could I not be moved as I watched Michel pick up his grandfather's drawing in his large hands? He walked over to the window and examined it in silence for several minutes. Was it the art expert or the grandson looking at the picture? It was dizzying to witness this encounter, which bore us back through time and across generations. Michel carefully replaced the drawing on its stand without a word. Who was he reserving his analysis for?

A few moments later, speaking on the phone to his son, Andrew, he described the Tiepolo as a "fine drawing." He said nothing to me.

Now it was my turn to examine the drawing, executed in brown wash and bister, a kind of ink made from soot.

I peered at the pen-and-ink sketch of a long-haired young man, seen from behind, wearing a tunic made of hide. His left elbow leans lightly against a rock, and his seated body is slightly inclined to one side. His face is half in profile, lacking detail but the body is carefully drawn. He carries two objects emblematic of his occupation, a goatskin flask and a wooden staff; there is no landscape or animal in the background. The drawing is the pure distillation of its subject.

I had somehow hoped that the drawing might tell me something about Jules. But the shepherd turned away from me, withdrew, hid from any interpretation. I found myself particularly drawn to the boy's sketchy features. He reminded me of a line from a poem by Verlaine: "There was nothing fixed or settled about him . . ." His mystery was part of who he was.

The collector's mark on the drawing was not that of Jules but of Pierre Geismar, from whom Jules had purchased it in 1928. I looked for some trace of Jules; there was nothing written on the back of the drawing, but I noted one discreet clue—a white-and-gold mount or an intermediate frame, called in French, appropriately enough, a "marie-louise," that he had picked out over eighty years before.

XVI

ALONE IN PARIS, 1940

Nadine entrusted me with a long letter from Marie-Louise, with the occasional contribution by Jules, composed between early October and early November 1940. I spent hours deciphering Marie-Louise's small, sloping script and putting the sheets of pale blue, semi-transparent onionskin paper in order.

It was addressed from 60 Avenue Foch to her daughters Élisabeth and Françoise, who had recently moved to the Free Zone in the south with Élisabeth's husband and children.

What a joy it was to discover this account by Marie-Louise and Jules, to touch the very paper they had written on, to hear their voices at last. The strength of the bonds between the various family members, their material concerns in wartime, the straightforward way they addressed one another, came across very powerfully. As I read, I felt a great deal of admiration for Marie-Louise. I was keenly aware of her courage and her determination to supply her daughters with whatever she thought they might need.

"I feel so depressed sometimes at the memory of all the things we have lost," writes Marie-Louise. "I can't help thinking how careless I was, and I blame myself." What "things" was she thinking of? Could she perhaps have been referring to the art that was stolen from the family? In what way did she feel she had been careless? Careless for failing to see that war was imminent? Careless in terms of the decisions she had made?

She hopes the things she has sent her daughters are useful. She hasn't been able find pajamas, so she has sent them some fabric instead. She did manage to find butter, even if it was a touch rancid, but no chocolate this time. Jules doesn't leave the house much anymore. The doctor comes to see him at home. Their circle of friends is shrinking.

It's clear she is beginning to feel deep anxiety, though she doesn't appear yet to grasp the magnitude and gravity of the situation. She assures her daughters that she is doing her best not to give into fear. She is desperate to hold on to normal life; she wants for nothing, she tells them, everything will be fine, though she does tend to worry. She has the odd friend over for a meal, and she must confess she misses her games of bridge.

She is so proud of my father, Philippe, and his studies. She has sent him books and bonbons.

The well-being of her family is at the heart of Marie-Louise's concerns. But beneath the urge not to bother their daughters with their parents' problems, Marie-Louise and Jules's unhappiness at being alone in Paris is palpable. They are worried about their grandson Claude, of whom they have had no news for two months. There is no mention of André, or of their little grandson Michel, who is now in the United States with his mother. Nothing is said directly about the war or the Germans. When Jules writes, it is to complain of how expensive life has become, that "dairymen, butchers, and bakers" can afford to wear mink now; this comes across not so much as snobbery but as grief at seeing their world disappearing before their eyes.

Marie-Louise is relieved that Élisabeth seems "calm and content," even happy, with her family in Aix. She hopes she will have a good influence on her younger sister, Françoise who, far from her husband, her eldest son, and her Parisian friends, is anxious and adrift.

Jules is fatigued and depressed, suffering from a sickness both mental and physical. He has almost stopped leaving the apartment since the elevator stopped working. He plays Patience in the evening. The only thing that seems to lift his spirits is their regular Sunday jaunt to have lunch at La Crémaillère, the high point of their week. (Even today, the importance of food as a source of comfort and pleasure remains much in evidence in the family. At the age of ninety-one, Nadine still enjoys cooking, and doesn't think twice about crossing Paris by taxi to try out a new restaurant.)

Jules writes a brief snatch of poetry that testifies to his sorrow and apprehension:

"What has become of the beautiful days of yesteryear, the quays of the Seine, and the nightingales? Shall we ever know them again?"

Perhaps in implicit response to his wife's self-reproach,

Jules, in a tone that seems infused with both wisdom and disillusion, tries to offer solace to his daughter Françoise:

"My darling, it is absolutely vital to maintain a sense of calm, and not indulge in regret, what you should or should not have done. No one can tell you what to do, you must follow your instincts, for better or for worse."

This final sentence in Jules's hand is dated November 1940. Neither he nor Marie-Louise indicates that they have moved or are planning to, though their move must have taken place around this time.

Reading the letter, I felt enormous sadness for the weary and despondent Marie-Louise and Jules. What made them choose to stay on in Paris rather than join their daughters in Aix? I tried to imagine what it must have been like to be in my great-grandmother's shoes, caring for Jules in occupied Paris with no one to lean on. I admired her strength and resilience and sensed her loneliness. I was reminded yet again of the frequently unenviable lot of women. We remember the artists, but we completely forget the women who struggle in the shadows, often single-handedly, to bring up their children and feed and care for their families.

I'd asked Nadine, reread Michel's memoir, but I still had no idea why Jules and Marie-Louise left Avenue Foch. All I could gather was that the apartment was too big for them. I was not convinced. In occupied Paris, where the first anti-Jewish laws had been decreed in October 1940, no one moved house without a reason.

XVII

THE LOOTED ART ARCHIVES

On a bright, cold morning on May 1, 2017, I met Emmanuelle Polack for the first time, the art historian whose name I had first come across in Rachel Kahn's documentary about looted art. I had reached out to her after seeing it and she suggested we meet. She was holding a small bouquet of lilies of the valley, the traditional symbol of the workers' May Day holiday in France. I was touched by the gesture and by her warm, cheerful demeanor. I liked her immediately.

She was aware of who Jules was. Without any preamble, she asked whether he had been deported. "He wasn't," I told her. "He died in Paris, in 1943, either of illness or old age." Even as I said these words, I was astonished once more at how little I really knew.

Before I brought up the subject of the Tiepolo drawing, I handed her a book I'd picked up, quite by chance, in a secondhand bookstore: *My Paris and Its Parisians,* published in 1954, in which the author, André de Fouquières, a self-described "worldly polymath," explores the neighborhood around the Place de l'Étoile and its denizens.

Monsieur Jules Strauss lived in an apartment at number 60, a veritable museum. He owned a splendid collection of paintings by Degas, Pissarro, Jongkind, Boudin, Whistler, Roussel, Carrière, a Delacroix *Crucifixion of Christ*, Courbet's *La Dormeuse* (*Sleeping Girl*), and a portrait of Berthe Morisot by Manet. When the collection was sold in 1932, Alfred Cortot acquired the portrait of Wagner, a copy of which was bequeathed by a certain Monsieur Chéramy to Paris's Opéra Museum—the only portrait of Wagner known to have been painted from life.

Michel had sent me a second photograph of Jules's study, showing it from the other side, with a different wall covered in yet more works of art. Emmanuelle examined the picture, expressing particular admiration for the one that Fouquières mentions, Manet's famous portrait of Berthe Morisot with a muff.

"This picture is very well known. Do you think it might have been stolen by the Germans?" she asked.

"As far as I know, most of these paintings were sold at auction in 1932. But it turns out that my grandmother put in a claim after the war for ten stolen paintings. I don't know why," I told her. "But I've found a drawing by Tiepolo which definitely did belong to Jules and is now in the Louvre."

I handed her a document and she read through it intently.

"I suggest that you don't put in a claim without having gathered as much evidence as you can lay your hands on," she said. "You really need a complete dossier. Do you know if the family made a claim through Rose Valland's commission after the war?"

I shook my head. "I have no idea."

"If your family did have paintings stolen, there is a good chance that you'll find something in the Looted Art Archives at La Courneuve. I'm going tomorrow morning. Why don't you meet me there at nine?"

I would have liked to ask if she'd be interested in working for my family, but before I had the chance to suggest it she said, as though reading my thoughts, "You're going to have to do the research yourself. It's your family, your history."

I remembered Alexis Kugel's words about this kind of research becoming an obsession. All of a sudden, for some reason, I no longer felt apprehensive at the thought of losing myself in this quest, of committing all my time and energy to it. Without even asking what kind of archive it was, I agreed to meet her there the next day. She was going to be my guide, my guardian angel.

I dropped the girls at school and took the RER, the suburban train, from Port-Royal to La Courneuve, a suburb some way out of Paris. I got off the train, feeling like I was in the middle of nowhere. I followed a sign pointing in the direction of the Foreign Ministry's Diplomatic Archives Center, and found myself in front of a high, sheer wall. There was a large security gate, then another. The pared-down opulence of the building, with its up-to-the-minute fittings and discreet security personnel, not to mention its size and its cavernous entrance hall, made it quite clear that this was an important site, designed to impress. I was filled with a yawning sense of futility. Was it really possible I was going to find the answers to all my questions inside this building?

After going through several security barriers to register and leaving my belongings in the cloakroom—I was allowed to take in only a notebook and a pencil (no pens in case they leaked and damaged a document)—at last I was allowed upstairs to the reading room. Emmanuelle had already arrived and settled down to work. There was a large dossier open on her desk. When she saw me, she stood up to show me around, explaining in a whisper how to find my bearings. She showed me the section of the archive with shelves labeled 209 SUP, the classification code for dossiers relating to looted art claims by families. If a French family had declared an object or a painting stolen, whatever its value, this is where written evidence of the claim would be found. Details of looted works of art recovered after the war whose owners cannot be traced are also filed here. One can search either according to the title of the work or by family name.

Emmanuelle was enthusiastic, energetic, reassuring, and completely at ease in this place that was so foreign to me. If she hadn't suggested I go with her and offered to be my guide, I might well have turned right around again and left.

I had the familiar sense of incongruity that had struck

me before in other archives, between the imposing architecture and the impressive and sleek interiors, and the sense of futility at the sight of the tiny number of researchers working there. What was the point of such a massive, expensive building if only a few people cared?

I pulled down from a shelf an inventory of all the claims made to the French Looted Art Commission and took it back to my desk. A dizzying list of hundreds of names, in no particular order. I recognized some, including Gunzbourg, like Aline and Antoinette; Wormser, like the great friends of Jules and Marie-Louise; David-Weill, the surname of my childhood friend Agathe, scion of a family of wealthy bankers, collectors, and patrons. Jules, too, had been a banker until he retired at the age of fifty to devote himself to art. I wondered if he, too, had made his fortune in banking. Was it only wealthy Jewish families whose collections were stolen? I scrolled through these familiar names, perplexed. How could it be that I knew some of these families personally, and yet I'd never heard any mention of Nazi thefts?

I skimmed through the names. Polack, like Emmanuelle. Fabius, like Laurent, the former prime minister. My eyes blurred. I closed them for a moment. There were dozens more pages to look through. The lines were getting mixed up. My eyes hurt, my head hurt, but I pushed on. Suddenly I saw the name Strauss—but it was a Monsieur Émile Strauss, a different family altogether.

It occurred to me that this might not be the most efficient way of doing things. But then I realized that if there were people I knew here, friends of the family, then maybe . . . I had to carry on. I returned to the interminable list, running my finger along each line . . . Suddenly my finger stopped on a name before I even realized its significance. I read the previous line several times, then the line that came after, to be sure that my eyes weren't deceiving me. At last, my finger stopped under the name, I said it in a whisper:

"Madame Jules Strauss."

So there was a dossier here for a restitution claim filed by my great-grandmother. My discovery put an end to weeks of doubt: if Marie-Louise had filed a claim, that must mean that my family had had their art expropriated.

The wait for the dossier felt interminable. No more than a couple of hours had passed from when I had walked through the entrance to the moment I found her name, but time passes differently in the archives. I sat in the reading room, watching the other people there, since I had nothing better to do. A woman I had seen at the Louvre and the Musée d'Orsay was photographing pages with an old-fashioned camera. A few students were using their cellphones to take pictures of documents.

I shivered. It was chilly. I got up and went to the admissions desk, where I was told that the ventilation was regulated for conservation purposes. Two tables along from me I recognized the philosopher Élisabeth Badinter, who was making notes about a manuscript propped up on a special cushion so as not to damage it.

Everything seemed so painfully slow and arduous.

And then the box of documents was brought to my desk

and immediately my frustration melted away. I began looking through it, feverish with excitement, but I forced myself to calm down, because I knew I had to take enormous care handling these priceless documents.

Like an archaeologist seeing a treasure for the first time after months of excavation, I felt terribly emotional as I opened the box. The first document I took out was a certificate from the Tailleur & Son storage company declaring that the contents of the unit belonging to Jules and Marie-Louise Strauss had been seized by the "German authorities of Avenue d'Iéna."

There were sheets of paper with notes penciled in Marie-Louise's hand, apparently written in some haste.

There was the typewritten list of effects declared stolen by Marie-Louise from Tailleur & Son:

Inventory of furniture covered by our contract with
    Madame Strauss number 1468:
Furniture put into storage on 1st May 1941
1 occasional table, with 2 trays, the top one of which
    is scratched
1 large table
1 glass-fronted ebony cabinet
1 gilded end table, Louis XV (added in pencil)
1 crate of paintings

A total of 69 crates.
Removed by the German Services of Avenue d'Iéna,
54 Avenue d'Iéna 7th July 1942.

There was no mention of the Tiepolo drawing. An implausible sentence from Michel's memoir echoed in my mind: "They miraculously survived the war." This dossier, which had sat undiscovered for seventy years, was poignant testimony that the opposite was the case.

I think curiosity conquered emotion. I was trying to understand something about which no one had ever uttered a word to me. I scanned the list of stolen assets—chairs, tables, boxes of vanished silverware. I was intrigued by the last thing on the list, a "crate of paintings." How many paintings fit into a crate? At least two, presumably. Did Marie-Louise not know what her husband had put in the crate? Did it contain the Tiepolo drawing, before it was sold by Victor Mandl to Erhard Göpel? Under what circumstances had Jules placed all these things in storage, and how much had Marie-Louise known?

The "German Services of Avenue d'Iéna" could only be a reference to the ERR. I already knew that Rosenberg's organization had established its headquarters there.

Emmanuelle showed me the red and blue lines in the margin that indicated which pieces had been declared stolen. A few blue lines for the chairs and a large tapestry; the rest were red. Was this Rose Valland's own color code? Blue for recovered, red for the rest? Was it possible that Valland, who devoted her entire life to recovering the art stolen by the Nazis from French Jewish families, had actually gone through Marie-Louise's list herself?

I went over to the main desk to ask if the center kept copies of Nazi documents with details of the seizures from storage companies. With every new box that arrived at my desk after a forty-minute wait, my heart beat faster. I was hoping to find a list of specific pictures that had been put into storage. But I found nothing.

Both exhausted and filled with nervous energy, I went down to the cafeteria to gather my thoughts and have something to eat. The roller coaster of emotions, the glacial chill of the reading room, the endless waiting for documents to arrive, had all left me feeling ragged. My lunch was as horrible as it gets—a fridge-cold sandwich and a cup of instant soup from a machine—and yet I felt buoyant. I had never been so happy in my life. It was as if I could hear Marie-Louise's voice whispering in my ear, as if the seventy years that separated us had simply melted away.

XVIII

MY METHOD

I'd been invited to appear on a radio series about Degenerate Art, to be interviewed for the episode entitled "The Memory Wound." We were sitting in the small, dimly lit Radio France studio, and the producer asked me to read aloud the list of stolen possessions that Marie-Louise had filed with her claim.

"Objects seized from Tailleur & Son on 7th July 1942: 1 gilded end table, Louis XV (added in pencil) 1 glass-fronted ebony cabinet, one chair . . . " I should have refused. What was the point of divulging details of a private document; and anyway, who was going be interested in a list of furniture?

I interrupted myself. "Isn't this a bit dull?" Perhaps I was trying to stop myself giving into the tears that had started pricking my eyes in spite of myself. The producer was irritated, she was going to have to cut this when she edited the program. The presenter continued, "So, is the idea to try to put together a sort of imaginary museum of Jules Strauss's vanished collection?"

Again, she'd managed to move me to tears. What a lovely way of putting it. I wished I had come up with it myself.

"Yes," I said. "That's exactly what I want to do."

It would make a good title for the book I was yet to write, if André Malraux hadn't got there first. I thought about Orhan Pamuk's *The Museum of Innocence,* dedicated to the memory of his beloved wife. How amazing it would be to open the Jules Strauss Museum to house his collection, to put together an exhibition in homage to the great-grandfather I had never known.

I don't remember the presenter's other questions, except one that caught me a little off guard:

"How did you go about your research?"

I hesitated for a moment before replying.

"I started by looking into every possible lead, family history, all at the same time. I made lists of the works that had belonged to Jules and went through auction house archives to try and find out who'd sold them and when. I wrote to academics, art historians, other researchers, sociologists. All at the same time."

I wasn't sure my words would be any help to other families doing similar research. I'd have liked to offer some useful advice, suggest a strategy that could work for anyone, a step-by-step procedure. But the truth was I worked with a blend of instinct, enthusiasm, and curiosity. I was convinced everything was right there, just waiting to be discovered, and there's no method for that. The truth was, I was making it all up as I went along.

"I started this research in a very unfocused way, looking at it from every possible angle," I said. "Really, my method was that I had no method."

For several months I had been applying this idiosyncratic technique in the Foreign Ministry's Diplomatic Archives Center. Every morning I would drop the girls at school, walk to the station, and catch the train to La Courneuve. As the train went through the town of Drancy, where some seventy thousand French Jews were interned before being deported to Nazi death camps, I would always think of Roger Sorbac, murdered at Auschwitz.

Helena insisted on the importance of developing a research methodology, but I was very unconfident about my abilities. Too often I'd been told, "You're too disorganized, you need to be more rigorous." And yet here I was—I'd located the dossiers pertaining to my family and, for the first time in my life, I felt confident about what I was doing.

In my brilliant family—my great-grandfather with his exquisite taste; my father, a war hero who'd been high up in the civil service; my brothers, who between them cover a whole range of artistic talents—I've often felt left behind. For one thing, I'm a woman, and it is not by chance that my list of gifted relatives doesn't include a single woman—the women in my family have always remained in the shadows, their qualities often ignored. But here, in this Paris suburb, in this archive where no relative of mine has ever been, where no one was expecting me, and where I would never have imagined setting foot, I could finally be myself. There was no need to be brilliant or talented here. I found references for the relevant archival boxes, I filled in the consultation request forms, I waited patiently for the boxes to arrive. This was where I belonged.

Now that I had begun to go through the 209 SUP catalog of the Rose Valland archive, which contained Marie-Louise's claim, I realized that though I'd been questioning her about Jules for months, Nadine had told me very little about my great-grandmother. Marie-Louise was born in Paris, just after the 1870 Franco-Prussian war. Her mother was from England, born into a middle-class Jewish family of fabric merchants from Leeds. Marie-Louise, a fiercely independent young woman, intelligent, and even a little intimidating, was in no hurry to get married, and she kept Jules waiting a long time. She read widely in French, English, and German. Nadine claimed she favored the boys in the family. But she admired her fortitude: she told me that Marie-Louise was the only person who knew about André's terminal cancer diagnosis, which she kept completely to herself.

It was time for a proper look at the dozens of sheets of paper covered in her pretty copperplate, written in haste and attached to the original claim. I went through them one by one. Together they made up an impressive mosaic of stolen works. "Bronze mirror with birds, stolen from Avenue Foch," had been added in pencil to the list of "objects stolen late November 1941, 54 Avenue d'Iéna." A desk with drawers, a Louis XIV pendulum clock, a gold-embroidered daybed . . . Did she really believe she would recover them? I also found a copy of the contract with Tailleur, on which had been stamped a German eagle, with a penciled addition in the margin:

"Two Tailleur storage units, emptied on 7th July 1942."

The Strausses had managed to stay alive, but they appear to have been regularly dispossessed wherever they went.

I also found a dossier labeled "Strauss restitution," the correspondence between Jacques Dupont and a certain Monsieur Florisone. I recognized the name Dupont from the preface to the 1961 auction catalog that he had written in his capacity as president of the Society of the Friends of the Louvre, in which he paid homage to the memory of Jules and his gift of frames that lined the galleries of the Louvre. I now understood that he had been a member of the post-war Commission for the Recovery of Works of Art, working alongside Rose Valland. At the beginning of 1945, the two had traveled to the collection points in Germany where looted artworks discovered by American troops had been brought. Teams from the commission were charged with identifying the works and repatriating them to France.

Everything was falling into place. When he alluded to Jules's life under Nazi occupation—"During the terrible years of the Occupation, it was a difficult task to keep all these objects safe"—Dupont must have known that the Strauss collection had been plundered by the Germans. I realized he must have advised and aided the family after the war. I discovered that one painting had been returned to Marie-Louise: "Happy New Year! Painting by Canot, *returned to Madame Strauss in 1951*." It must have been Dupont himself who had intervened in person to ensure that the painting, classified as looted art by the MNR, was given back to my great-grandmother. It had been stolen by the *Möbel-Aktion* services from the Tailleur storage company's headquarters on July 7, 1942. Yet during the entire period I had been talking to Nadine and various cousins, not a single person had mentioned that this painting had been returned to the family.

Convinced that the Nazis must have kept some kind of written evidence, I decided to look into the archives of the *Möbel-Aktion*, only to be told that unfortunately most of the documents had been burned. Any that had survived were located in the German city of Koblenz.

XIX

THE KOBLENZ ARCHIVE

Emboldened by my discoveries at La Courneuve, and filled with a spirit of adventure, I decided on a whim to go with Emmanuelle Polack to Koblenz. We both wanted to visit the German Federal Archives branch holding Nazi documents pertaining to owners who had still not been identified, including photographs of hundreds of paintings confiscated from emptied apartments during the *Möbel-Aktion*.

Emmanuelle was doing research into the Gurlitt affair. Cornelius Gurlitt, the son of an art dealer who dealt in Nazi-looted art, was arrested on a train in 2010, in possession of an exceedingly large amount of cash. The German authorities discovered over a thousand works of art stashed in his apartment, most of it acquired during the war by his father, Hildebrand Gurlitt. Emmanuelle was part of a working group brought together by the German government to establish the works' provenance.

If the apartments on Avenue Foch and Avenue d'Iéna, as well as the storage unit, had indeed been looted, perhaps I would find a trace of my great-grandparents' stolen paintings in photographs held in Koblenz. Confident I would manage my way around the German archives just as I had in La Courneuve, I left for Germany, birthplace of my ancestors, filled with enthusiasm but woefully ill-prepared.

I booked an Airbnb apartment near the railway station and noted down the address of the archive. We took two trains, changing at Frankfurt, the city of Jules's birth. I regret now that I didn't break my journey there to visit the municipal archives and the cemetery, to see if I could find any trace of Jules's five brothers and sisters, and perhaps find out if I had any distant relatives still living there, but I was too impatient to get to Koblenz.

We were in such a hurry to investigate these new sources, Emmanuel for Gurlitt and I for the Strausses, that we headed straight for the archive with our luggage. We took two trains along the Rhine and a bus, then walked a few kilometers farther out from the center of town. At last we found ourselves at the ultramodern building that houses the federal archives. Half an hour later, we were sitting in front of the library's computer terminals. Disaster. The catalog was in German, the archives had not yet been digitized, and the librarian spoke barely any English.

In the search box, marked *Suche,* I tried typing in "Jules Strauss." Nothing. I tried all the search engines. No luck. Where and how was I supposed to look? I needed to find out how the documents were classified, but it was impossible to communicate with the librarian. I sat and watched Emmanuelle as she opened a large box of reproductions, each one marked on the back with an inventory number, the title of the painting, and the name of the artist. These were photographs taken in people's apartments during the *Möbel-Aktion,* whose owners had not yet been identified. As the photos, like everything else there, hadn't been digitized, Emmanuelle had to go through them one by one.

"Research takes time," said Emmanuelle, seeing my doubtful expression.

We went to the canteen. The food was so revolting I took photos to show Henri. After lunch I called the owner of the apartment.

"I'm sorry, the apartment isn't available this evening, there's been a mistake!" he said, explaining that he had rented the studio to someone else. There we were, in the Nazi archives, with our luggage and nowhere to sleep. Emmanuelle laughed, and off we set, dragging our suitcases through the streets of Koblenz in search of a hotel.

I don't recall anything much about those two days in Koblenz, as if I experienced them outside time and space. I barely knew where I was. I just remember the little restaurants with their embroidered placemats where, whatever we ordered, we were served sausages, fresh egg noodles, and giant pretzels. I don't recall seeing any salad or vegetables. Few people spoke English. There was some kind of trade show going on and all the hotels were full.

We walked and walked, asking in every hotel we passed, until we got to the river. The view over the water seemed brighter somehow, despite the slanting autumn light. At last, at dusk, we found a hotel with two rooms available looking out over the Rhine. We unpacked and went to the nearest bar, where we ordered pints of beer and laughed and laughed at our ridiculous situation.

When we got back to our rooms, I fell to thinking about my children, whom I'd left behind on a quest for something that was based entirely on conjecture. I felt so foreign in this country. Not that it seemed hostile, it was just that I had no bearings. I couldn't understand a thing, of either the language or the aesthetics.

In the evening the indefatigable Emmanuelle worked on her thesis on the art market during the Occupation. I crawled into bed, exhausted after the long day.

The next day, Emmanuelle picked up the pace; she needed to take photographs of the thirty-six reproductions before we left. Since I didn't really know what else to do, I copied her. I'd brought with me a list of fifty pictures that had at some point belonged to Jules, of which I hadn't a single image. I wasn't sure how to go about finding them. How many views of Venice had Guardi painted, how many roses in a vase were there by Renoir?

I watched Emmanuelle, doggedly continuing her task, excited by the discovery of these photographs in boxes marked *Unbekannt* or Unknown, intoxicated by all this new material.

"You have to be patient, Pauline, don't forget . . . research takes time."

She finished taking photographs and began flicking through files of correspondence. She told me she knew just enough German to find her way around. She translated one for me: "Exchanges between Victor Mandl and Erhard Göpel." We knew that the Tiepolo drawing had passed through the hands of both these men: Victor Mandl was a German-born antique dealer with a shop on rue Boccador, while Erhard Göpel worked for Hitler, acquiring art for the museum that the Führer was planning to build in Linz.

These were copies of files, with no explanatory material, and, frustratingly, no one to translate them for me. Instead, I took pictures of the documents. There was nothing else I could do.

A few days later I sent the photographs to Marius Mazotti, the German student who had already done some research for me in the Berlin archives. He had no difficulty translating the Gothic-style handwriting. He also had good news. Quite by chance, I had stumbled upon the receipt of the sale by Mandl to Göpel of Tiepolo's *A Shepherd,* irrefutable proof that it had been sold to the Nazis.

XX

THE TAILLEUR & SON STORAGE COMPANY

> *Paris, 5th March 1945*
> *I the undersigned, Philippe TAILLEUR, owner and manager of the Storage Company, TAILLEUR & Son, 106 rue du Bac, Paris, certify that the furniture belonging to Madame STRAUSS (Contract N.1564) was removed from storage by the German Services of Avenue d'Iéna on 7th July 1942.*
>
> *For and on behalf of the Storage Company Tailleur & Son.*
>
> *Director*
> *Philippe Tailleur*

I found out how brave Marie-Louise was from reading the long letter she had sent her daughters during the war. I imagined her, no less courageous, a few years later, gathering documents, hanging on to the hope of one day recovering some of her possessions.

She had lost three people very dear to her in just a few years: first her son, André, then her son-in-law Roger, and finally Jules. She had moved several times, in the course of which she seems to have lost virtually everything she owned. One day, in the spring of 1945, she went to see Monsieur Tailleur to ask him to supply her with written confirmation of the theft of her possessions, without which she had no chance of recovering anything.

I imagined her, dressed all in black, walking along the same street I go down almost every day. The Tailleur address, 106, rue du Bac, was familiar to me, but I was startled to realize that the place from which the Strausses' possessions had been stolen is now the Secours Catholique, the Christian charity where I often go to drop off old clothes.

I paused for a moment before the entrance, struck by the thought that it can be easier to wade through a dusty old folder of documents than to bring up the subject of Nazi war crimes with a stranger. But I was heartened by the familiar face of the man at the reception desk. "I wonder if you know anything about a storage company that used to occupy this building, about seventy years ago?" I asked him.

"A storage company?" He looked puzzled. I was painfully aware of the pitfalls of this line of questioning.

"My great-grandfather stored his furniture here during the war"—I hesitated a moment; either he would grasp what I was talking about, or he'd think I was some kind of madwoman come to claim stolen goods from half a century ago—"and the thing is, the whole lot was stolen." I didn't mention the word Nazi. I didn't want to scare him off.

He had no idea what I was talking about, and took me over to his colleague, who'd been working there for longer. This man had heard of Tailleur, and he led me out to the courtyard around which the old building, long since destroyed, had once stood.

I tried to piece it all together. In early 1941, the Tailleur truck would have driven the short distance from Avenue Foch to rue du Bac, and into the company's courtyard. Removal men would have taken out sixty-nine crates and carried them into a room on the ground floor. One of them would have been holding the inventory drawn up presumably by either Jules or Monsieur Tailleur and signed by Jules.

The following year, on July 7, 1942, men from the *Dienststelle Westen*, which ran the *Möbel-Aktion* and was head-quartered at 54 Avenue d'Iéna, would have entered the same building and ordered Monsieur Tailleur to unlock the storage units. Perhaps they ordered him to open those belonging to Jews first. Perhaps Jules Strauss was near the top of their list. Did they take everything or make a selection? There was a selection point on rue de Bassano, around the corner from Avenue d'Iéna. Is this where the crates were taken?

I knew frustratingly few facts. Which of Jules's paintings were in the crates? Where were the paintings taken? The furniture? Was it all auctioned at Drouot? Perhaps I was on the right track. I'd seen photos of the department store windows where stolen furniture was stored before being sent to Germany. But how could I possibly identify two French Regency chairs?

If the paintings had been taken from rue du Bac to the Jeu de Paume, they would have been recorded by Rose Valland and identified after the end of the war.

"Madame, is there anything else I can do for you?"

I'd been standing in the courtyard for ten minutes, lost in thought. I'd forgotten all about the man from reception, waiting for me to leave so that he could return to his desk.

"No, thank you, I'm fine," I assured him.

I didn't know where to turn now. It seemed as though none of the hypotheses I had concocted in my head had any basis in reality. Not a trace of Tailleur & Son remained. Not even the walls. Everything was gone.

During the weeks that followed, I continued searching for the Tailleur archives. A man who owns a store selling socks and hosiery, born on rue du Bac, told me he remembered seeing Tailleur removal trucks as a child in the 1960s. Fascinated by the history of the street where he was born, he sat me down in his storeroom to show me a short film he'd made of bills and receipts from some of its long-gone storekeepers. His wife sat and watched it with us. Afterward I told them about my research into the lives of Jules and Marie-Louise. I showed them the photograph of their art-filled drawing room. The wife was intrigued. She told me she was related to Renoir. I thought for a moment she was joking, but she led me a few meters over the road into a courtyard from where we could just catch a glimpse of his studio. I didn't find out any more details about how she was related to Renoir, but I was moved by the unexpected encounter. Henri always teases me for saying how rare it is that we really talk to people. Yet had it not been for my investigation we'd never have had this conversation, even though we had briefly interacted dozens of times before.

Perhaps the Tailleur archives would give up some secrets. I looked through the *Pages Blanches,* the directory of Paris professionals, and found a Jean Tailleur. I called but got the answering machine. Did I really think he was going to call back and tell me, "Yes, that's my grandfather, I kept everything, you're welcome to come and look through the archives whenever you like"?

I didn't even bother to leave a message.

Tailleur & Son had been bought out by a removal company called Demeco in the 1970s. I called the company headquarters, but they weren't very cooperative. "Archives? No idea...Who might you ask? No idea." I tried various other numbers but came up with nothing. Had everyone who worked there been told not to reveal anything about this less than glorious period of their history?

There had certainly been plenty of work for removal companies during the war, emptying the apartments of deported Jews. But did that mean one had to suspect every removal company of collaboration?

I called the removers' trade association. No one knew whom to ask. They promised to call me back.

Back at the National Archives in Pierrefitte, I looked through details of lawsuits brought against removal companies. I found a file on the Grospiron removal company, whose trucks still ply the streets of Paris. There was no mention of the Strausses. I had another look at some files relating to the "German services of Avenue d'Iéna"—which I now knew for sure was the ERR, the Rosenberg task force. What a strange irony of history that the ERR had been headquartered in the very building where Jules and Marie-Louise had taken refuge.

The Tailleur trail was turning out to be more complex that I'd thought. I needed to locate the archives and work out what exactly was in the crates stored there by Jules and Marie-Louise.

XXI

SUDDENLY, MODIANO

Henri had been nagging me for weeks to talk to Patrick Modiano about my research. Patrick and I had known each other for years, though not particularly well, and I hesitated to bother him; I was rather shy around this man I admired so much. I actually carry around with me the speech he gave when he was awarded the Nobel Prize for Literature in 2014. I often think about what he said then about belonging to a generation of children who were "seen and not heard," who were constantly interrupted by adults who didn't know how to listen to them. His own desire to write arose from the urge to get adults to "listen to you without interrupting and they will certainly know what it is you have on your chest."

One Sunday morning a flea market was taking place in our neighborhood. We were milling among the stands when Henri spotted the unmistakable tall, slightly stooped, gray-haired figure of the great writer, wearing his signature raincoat and walking alongside his petite, vivacious wife. Of course, it was out of the question that I would flag him down in the street.

I was born two streets away, and I know the neighborhood like the back of my hand; if I ran I could get to Boulevard

Raspail and reach the intersection with rue de Varenne just in time to make it seem as though I had bumped into the Modianos by chance. I knew how reserved Patrick was and that he would no doubt hate to be approached like this. Too bad. I ran as fast as could; there was something I wanted to ask him that had been plaguing me for weeks. I wouldn't get another chance like this.

I stopped a few meters ahead of him to catch my breath and regain my composure. He didn't seem in the least surprised to see me. Nor did he appear to notice that I was pink-cheeked, slightly short of breath, and trembling slightly at my audacity. I could have addressed him by his first name, but I didn't dare. I looked at his wife, Dominique, and addressed them both, cheered on by her friendly smile.

"Hallo!" I groped for the right formula to introduce myself but came up with nothing. Instead, a little abruptly, I said, "I'm doing some research into my great-grandfather, the art collector Jules Strauss. I'm trying to find out what happened to him during the war, and I've been wondering if I might talk to you."

He looked at me with a kindly expression, as though I'd said something totally unremarkable, as if I'd asked him for directions, or if he had the time.

"Jules Strauss, the great collector, of course. I believe he lived in the building owned by the Phoenix insurance company. Sixty Avenue Foch, if I'm not mistaken."

I was utterly taken aback. How did he know where my great-grandfather had lived seventy years ago? Once again, the name Jules Strauss was like an open sesame. I stood there in stunned silence, smiling in agreement, not daring to interrupt.

"The Nazis requisitioned the apartment. I think I have something about it among my papers, but I'm not sure." He gestured broadly with one hand, as if about to plunge once more into the abyss of the past, where everything is opaque and complicated. Even so, he seemed to know about it in quite some detail.

I had tears in my eyes. In an instant, he had conjured Jules and his story into existence.

I had long suspected that the reason Jules and Marie-Louise had moved had nothing to do with their apartment being too large for the two of them. And now this chance encounter with Modiano provided me with a pivotal piece of evidence: the Strausses had indeed been driven out of Avenue Foch by the Nazis. I was devastated; Jules and Marie-Louise had suffered far more than I had realized.

I felt an unexpected fraternity with this great writer; we were from the same world, where people dig into the past, for whom the past is always there, sometimes more present than the present itself.

He promised to look through his papers and see what he could find. Shaken, I gave him my phone number and turned to go.

A few weeks later I was in Normandy, sitting by the pool, when the phone rang.

"Good afternoon, this is Patrick Modiano. I do hope I'm not disturbing you."

It was too bad that my daughters barely knew how to swim, and that the ninety-year-old gentleman who was our guest for the weekend was likely not sprightly enough to keep an eye on them. I grabbed a piece of paper from my purse to note down what Modiano told me. In his low, almost timorous voice, he recounted the details of the requisitioning of Jules's apartment. I finally had the answer to the question that had been nagging me for weeks.

"An agent of the *SD*, the Gestapo security services, by the name of Kurt Maulaz, moved into your great-grandparents' apartment in 1940. He was part of the Otto network, and entertained many members of Parisian high society who collaborated with the Germans, at least financially: the Boussac family, Jean de Beaumont, and others. I've got all the details among my papers, if you're interested in knowing more."

As I listened, I conjured up images of parties thrown by Maulaz in my great-grandparents' apartment. Marc Masurovsky would later describe Maulaz to me as "a typical SD agent, ruthless, selfish, in complete thrall to Nazi ideology. A zealot. And highly efficient." Images spooled through my mind like a bad movie: beautiful women, wealthy French industrialists, Nazis, collaborators, champagne. All this in their drawing room, among Jules's paintings and sculptures. While he was being persecuted, humiliated, robbed.

This was how I imagined it, but the reality was I still knew very little, even though thanks to Modiano my research had taken a huge leap. Jules and Marie-Louise had not made it through the war unscathed, there had been no miracle, as Michel had hoped. Another stone cast into the deep well of my family's silence and denial.

I invited Michel, who was in Paris for a few days, to come and see my brother Édouard perform in an adaptation of Modiano's autobiographical novel *A Pedigree* at the Théâtre Antoine. As we walked through the foyer, I was startled to realize that this was the very theater where Simone Berriau had been director when she purchased Degas's drawing of the little schoolboy from Jules. This was just the first coincidence of the evening.

Watching my brother bring Modiano's character to life, recounting stories about his parents during the Occupation and his childhood after the war—his father's shady activities on the black market, the Boussac family, Jean de Beaumont, it was all there—I wondered if the power of his performance might partly be explained by something in his own history.

I glanced at Michel, wondering what he thought of Édouard's performance, and how much he knew of the similarities with certain aspects of what had happened to our family. He'd fallen asleep. Henri, seated on his other side, was almost in tears, as was I by the end, when the young man Modiano finds himself at last able to breathe, the burden of the past having lifted and given way to hope:

"That evening, I felt a lightness of being for the first time in my life. The feeling of dread that had been weighing me down for all these years, forcing me to be constantly on the alert, evaporated in the Paris air. I'd managed to get away just before the worm-ridden pontoon collapsed. It was time."

XXII

COLD FEET

My feet were soaked. I'd been standing on the wet grass for two hours, repeating the same thing over and over again in different formulations:

"Here we are, on Avenue Foch, nicknamed 'Avenue of the Gestapo' during the Occupation because the Germans requisitioned a dozen buildings on this street. My great-grandparents lived at number sixty, until the Nazis requisitioned their apartment and they were forced to move out."

I'd recently found out about the long list of Nazi organizations that had been based in the Strausses' apartment building, which I was awkwardly reciting to camera. I'd agreed to take part in a television documentary about professionals and amateurs, like me, researching looted assets. The cameraman was filming, the director was reading her notes, the sound technician was wielding the boom with an absent expression on his face. It was gray, cold, and damp. I felt truly dejected. Why was I recounting my family history to total strangers?

"Could you do it again, but turning this way? I'd like you to cross the street and point toward the building. Take it a little more slowly. From the top, please."

I was irritated by them all, particularly the director's over familiar tone.

I started again. "The apartment was requisitioned by an SD agent named Kurt Maulaz—oh, I'm sorry, no, he was an agent of the Gestapo security services, head of the economic service, who dealt with the Otto lists, forbidden books. And was also responsible for . . ."

I couldn't remember what Maulaz's role was. I had to stop. I was useless at history, and I'd forgotten to print out the Gestapo organization chart. I knew I didn't sound interesting, my heart just wasn't in it. I kept looking up at the apartment, trying to work out which were the windows of Jules's study.

Then I saw him. He walked to the window but didn't open it. His handsome, sad eyes were framed by a pair of round spectacles, like the ones worn by Léon Blum. I'd have given anything to have been able to speak to him.

He was such a private, discreet person, and here I was discussing his life for a television program. The more I said, the more I realized that I knew nothing about who he really was. I imagined I was going to visit him and Marie-Louise, across the lobby, up five flights of stairs, through their front door and into the grand entrance hall, down the corridor to the double reception room, into Jules's study, with its walls lined with paintings.

The cameraman interrupted my reverie.

"Would you mind starting again from the top? Coming through the gate, please."

He smiled, pleased with his concept, the woman pushing open the gate as she talked about the Nazis. It was more modern.

Jules hadn't even been deported, which was a little disappointing, so there would be no tears in my close-up.

When were they going to ask me questions? I'd had enough talking to the camera, worrying about my hair and whether my nose looked big at this angle. Discreetly, I sent Nadine a text message. She'd lived here with her grandparents, from 1932 to 1939. She was the only person who could help me: "Nadine, did Jules and Marie-Louise live at number fifty-eight or number sixty? Sixty is a more beautiful building. You mentioned an ornate façade, so I wasn't sure." My phone rang almost immediately. It was Nadine, I had to answer. We spoke for a couple of minutes, then I said to the cameraman apologetically:

"I'm sorry, I got it wrong. Jules Strauss lived next door." He looked extremely irritated at the prospect of doing it all over again since I had been facing toward number fifty-eight while they filmed earlier. I was going to have to go through my monologue once more. I was freezing. I begged the director for a coffee break.

"No, we don't have time, Pauline. Do you think you could walk and talk at the same time? What about trying it as you enter the building? You could ring the bell for the fifth floor. That would add a bit of drama."

This time I smiled. I didn't need to ring the bell to enter the building.

That evening, I sent the director an email:

"Lætitia, I'm so sorry, but I don't want to be in the documentary, I'm not ready to publicize my research, which is very personal. To be honest, I've found the filming, the fact of talking about my family, quite grueling. I realize I'm complicating things for you by pulling out. But I just can't do it. I'm truly sorry."

I thought this email was my escape, though I knew it was more a case of emotional cowardice than discretion. Guiltily, I thought of the other families whose possessions had been looted by the Nazis, who might have found my experiences helpful.

XXIII

"MY STRENGTH WAS DISCRETION"

By the end of May 2017, I'd found a list of paintings declared stolen during the war that appeared to have already been sold; evidence of a crate of as yet unidentified paintings taken from a storage unit during the war; and a Tiepolo drawing whose provenance I was still trying to establish. I had no idea how to proceed from here.

Oddly, in the face of such uncertainty, the idea of going to see a clairvoyant seemed perfectly logical. I'd been to consult Nadège once before, but she didn't remember me. Perhaps if one has the gift of seeing into both the past and the future, one doesn't need a good memory.

The first time I'd gone to see her was to ask what to do with my life. I was forty and beginning to be seriously concerned that I still hadn't published anything. I was hoping she might detect in me a mysterious vocation or buried talent. She didn't seem to have picked up anything in particular, but her words encouraged me not to give up hope. Perhaps that was the reason I decided to go back and see her now. I was feeling forlorn and confused. I needed more encouragement that I was on the right path.

I sat in the vestibule, wracked with anxiety. Was I going to uncover some ghastly family secret? There was no reason to think the family was made up only of heroes. There could well have been traitors, cowards, or figures who were, at the very least, ambiguous. I wasn't sure I really wanted to find out. And if I told the bureaucrats in charge of the National Museums Artwork Recovery Division or the curators at the Louvre that a clairvoyant had "seen" the Tiepolo in the Strausses' drawing room, would this be enough to persuade them finally to return it to us?

I was frightened of what she would see. And terrified she would see nothing at all.

Nadège welcomed me into her consulting room. Dressed all in white, with bleached blond hair and a generous bosom, she had a warm, friendly demeanor, nothing like the stereotype of a fortune-teller. Without a word, I handed her the two photographs. I'd decided to avoid the words "Jew" and "looted art"; I didn't want to make her job too easy.

The first photograph was the one taken in the early 1920s of a dapper-looking Jules with hat, cane, and cigarette. The other was the one of Jules's study.

She didn't simply look at the pictures. She absorbed herself in them for several minutes, before raising her eyes and asking, "Was he a collector? I see an historian—no, an art historian—helping you. A woman."

Oh dear. I'd been hoping to avoid the whole "I see, I see," thing. Was she "seeing" Emmanuelle Polack?

She also "saw" the countries where I needed to orient my

research: the Netherlands, Switzerland, and Germany. She spoke of paintings sold in the United States. Later, she said, I was going to continue my search in museums and archives all over the world.

And then she said she could hear Jules talking to me. A shiver went down my spine and I put aside all my critical faculties when she uttered Jules's words:

"Be the light that illuminates the dark path."

I felt the urge to laugh, but at the same time I really did want to believe that Jules was tasking me with this mission. Even if it wasn't really Jules speaking, somehow these words reassured me that I wasn't doing all this for nothing. I decided to take what she said at face value.

"Yes, he is telling you to unveil the repressed family secrets," she went on.

Jules would have had no truck with such pseudo-psychological notions. I felt slightly ashamed to be getting his memory mixed up with the words of someone who was in all likelihood nothing but a charlatan.

But what Nadège said next was extraordinary. She said she saw Jules contacting an art-loving German officer. I suggested a few names I'd come across in the course of my research. The first was Kurt von Behr who, in his capacity as head of the ERR in France, was known to have sometimes helped himself to works of art. I mentioned Behr's assistant, Bruno Lohse, who, having deposited several stolen paintings in a safe in Zurich, became an art dealer after the war in Munich. By the end of 1941 both men had offices at

54 Avenue d'Iéna, where I now knew for sure that Jules and Marie-Louise had moved in 1941. The third name I gave her was Kurt Maulaz, the SD agent Modiano had told me about, who had been based at 60 Avenue Foch, almost certainly in the Strausses' apartment, though I was yet to lay my hands on any definitive evidence. The fourth name I put forward was the German ambassador, Otto Abetz.

None of these names meant anything to her, but she spoke of a strong link with an officer who had protected the family. Without the knowledge of his superiors, he had tried to propose a deal to Jules.

What made this extraordinary was that not long before, Andrew and I had met for lunch with Nadine, and Andrew had brought up a theory that was so fascinating and disturbing, so novelistic, it made my hair stand on end: What if Jules, who'd been born in Germany, had met an art-loving German officer and negotiated his family's survival and escape, and his own relative safety during the Occupation, in exchange for works of art? Our aunt thought this was far-fetched; It seemed obvious to her that a Nazi dignitary would have had no need to negotiate a deal when he could simply have taken whatever he wanted. I didn't see how we could ever know one way or the other, unless we were to discover some secret correspondence between the two men in a private German archive, or a great-grandchild who, like me, was studying the history of one of his forebears. Yet here was the medium, putting forward exactly the same theory.

She mentioned an argument between Jules and his

son-in-law, who accused Jules of negotiating with the enemy. This must have been Roger, before he was deported in 1942 on the first convoy out of France.

Nadège didn't quiver or speak with a strange voice. She was so artless that often I didn't know whether it was she who was speaking or Jules. She looked at the photograph of Jules again. Her face was cloaked with an expression of compassion and sorrow.

"Oh! This man was treated so badly."

Awful images jostled in my head. I asked Nadège if the eighty-year-old Jules had been beaten or threatened, mentally or physically. She didn't know.

"There were many French people who informed on their neighbors." That I knew. Did she have names, contexts? No. She swiftly changed the subject. "Was there a musician in the family?" she asked. "I sense someone close to Jules with a musical gift."

I wondered if this could be Marie-Louise. Later, I called Nadine, and she confirmed that Marie-Louise had indeed been a talented pianist. For some reason she had never mentioned this before. Truly, the qualities of the women in this family are all too often overlooked.

"Truth is only possible when history is acknowledged."

Was this an allusion to the difficulty the French had in recognizing the crimes of the Vichy government? How I wished she would speak normally. These Delphic utterances were not very helpful. The problem was I didn't know if it was Nadège who was speaking or Jules speaking through her.

Nadège intoned, *"I betrayed no one."*

At these words, I was overcome with a feeling of tremendous sadness. What accusation was Jules defending himself against? Who was he addressing? I know that people had become informers for money, but was this a reference to something specific I didn't know about? I wondered again about the circumstances of Roger's arrest on December 12, 1941.

Nadège continued. She said Jules had bought the survival of his family by giving away works of art. Maybe I'd given her the idea, but I was happy to go along with the game.

"Human folly makes us into vulgar traders," she went on, a grave expression on her face.

She seemed far away, as though plunged into a parallel world. I don't know if she was listening to a single voice, or sensing an entire realm.

"Learn to free yourself from the chains of the past. Think critically about history."

If this was Jules speaking to me, that was one thing, but if it was Nadège . . . I felt slightly aggrieved at the thought that she was lecturing me. I didn't know what to think. Some of what she came out with rang true.

"My strength was discretion and a gift for negotiation."

Jules had indeed been known for his discretion. When I looked at the black-and-white photograph of him, I could quite imagine him saying that.

"Now he is speaking of the brutality of men," said Nadège. *"I was never a barbarian. Victory was a matter of surviving the horror."*

Preoccupied by the negotiation theory, I tried to imagine all the possible scenarios that might have brought Jules and a German officer together. What words might have passed between them, what would the atmosphere have been— could there have been threats?

I told Nadège about the paintings Jules had put in storage with Tailleur & Son. She didn't react, but stared intently at the photo of Jules's study. She said I was going to have to go to Argentina. Did she mean Buenos Aires, where Roger's brother, Claude, had gone to live after the war? One day I was going to have to work out how to get him to talk properly.

"Why am I the one who's got caught up in all this?" I asked.

"Because you are the embodiment of neutrality." I didn't feel neutral, I felt filled with love and loyalty for my great-grandparents.

According to Nadège, my research was a way of cleansing the three generations that preceded mine, and the three that came after. I felt utterly incapable of helping so many people.

She returned to the family. "They managed to escape," she told me. I knew that most of the family had left, but I didn't know in what conditions, or the risks they had taken. All I knew was that when she was seventeen Nadine and Élisabeth had left France, making their way over the Pyrenees by foot and crossing into Spain, where they were placed under house arrest. Nadine had recounted snatches of this journey a thousand times, the only wartime episode that I sensed had caused her real suffering. Meanwhile my father had spent two months in prison in Spain before joining General Philippe Leclerc's Free French forces in Algeria.

At the end, I asked Nadège where I should begin my research. She suggested I begin with a list of paintings. Always the same mystery, the list of paintings claimed by my grandmother, not one of which appeared to have actually been stolen. Each time, back to the beginning, start all over again. I couldn't give up now.

XXIV

A COLLECTOR'S NOTEBOOKS

Michel was in Paris to catch up on some exhibitions. He brought over with him two notebooks that he'd inherited from Marie-Louise.

One was a small, plain notepad, dated 1931, handwritten and bound in vellum. The discolored pages were coming loose. The other was a small binder, also covered in vellum, in better condition, filled with typewritten pages, and dated 1941. Both bore Jules's signature.

Tiny tatters of paper flew out when I opened the notepad. The brittle, yellowing pages were filled with Jules's long, looping copperplate, with penciled notes in the margins, annotations in different colored inks, and entire passages struck through. It was difficult to make sense of it.

I read and reread the introduction as if it held some secret message that eluded me:

I have endeavored to relate here everything I know about my paintings, not glossing over any details. My observations are often the result of very lengthy research, verified by both French and foreign connoisseurs.

> *When it comes to art, only one thing counts: the pursuit of truth.*
>
> Errare humanum est! *But I plead good faith.*
>
> > *Jules Strauss, January 1931*

Who were these words addressed to? Did he imagine his notes would survive him? Why was "the pursuit of truth" so important to him? What kind of truth was he after—about the paintings, their histories, their origins? Who was he writing for? His family, posterity? Future collectors? Did he ever imagine that one day his great-granddaughter would read this, as she tried to find out his story?

Michel offered to lend me the notebooks, so that I could photocopy them before they fell apart completely. I was touched and surprised in equal measure. If they had been mine, I would have hesitated to let them out of my sight.

That evening, in my husband's office, I positioned each page on the glass of the photocopier. I was trembling, terrified of damaging them. I kept stopping to reread Jules's words.

He'd listed every painting he had owned, detailing the materials and format of each work, from whom it had been purchased, everything he knew about its former owners, and which exhibitions and books it had figured in. Successive corrections and notes in the margins testify to his immense intellectual curiosity, and the dates indicated that he had continued his investigations right up until his death. It was, I realized, the work of a genuinely erudite collector, in quest of full provenance, and this meant it should be possible to identify every work he had ever bought or sold.

The notebook was not so much a collector's notebook as a diary, in which Jules described each of his discoveries as faithfully as possible. He kept it on him always, as a painter might carry a sketchbook, or a writer a notebook to jot down ideas for a future novel. Not a day passed when he didn't add a detail or piece of information. It offers a moving insight into the thoughts of a man who never considered his research complete. Until this point, all I'd read was his catalogs; now I saw the increasingly tremulous handwriting of an aging man shoring up his knowledge against the fear of forgetting.

"Purchased with Roger Sorbac, repaid, sold." The story of a collector's life.

As I read on, I came across annotations that hinted at various crises. "Sold in 1941." I wondered what dramas might be hidden behind these words. Sometimes in the right-hand margin there was the word "stolen," or "MISSING," in thick red pencil alongside a reference to Tiepolo's *A Shepherd*. I couldn't tell if Jules had written this, or someone else. I asked Nadine, who told me it was Marie-Louise's handwriting. Long after her husband's death, when she registered the theft of the paintings, Marie-Louise must have gone through the notebooks to verify what was missing. Here at last was evidence that the Tiepolo had indeed disappeared from Jules's collection.

Jules left more than the memory of a collection in these notebooks: they are a mine of information, still useful for a collector, as well as an act of generosity, and a testament to a true love of art.

I think he would have liked them to be shared.

However, Elizabeth Royer, an independent provenance researcher, sounded a note of caution.

We had put in a claim for the return of the Tiepolo drawing from the Louvre, and a curator had asked to see Jules's notebooks. Elizabeth warned me against it.

"Whatever you do, don't give them the notebooks," she told me over the phone.

"Why not?" I didn't understand why she was so wary.

"You don't know what they're looking for."

"But what risk could there be?" I was genuinely puzzled.

"You're very naïve!" was her curt response.

For over twenty years Elizabeth has been working with families, helping them locate and recover artworks confiscated by the Nazis. In the basement of her beautiful Paris apartment she keeps copies of documents from looted art archives all over the world. She has dealt with the claims of over a hundred families, involving thousands of stolen paintings. I've often wondered how she finds the strength to wage these battles almost single-handedly. She isn't Jewish, and her family did not have their belongings looted during the war, yet she has devoted her life to this fight for justice. There's something mysterious and quixotic about her. Though I was filled with both admiration and gratitude for her commitment to her crusade, I also had a faint reservation about her propensity to hotheadedness.

We originally met after my cousin Andrew mentioned Jules to her two years earlier, and over time we developed a courteous relationship. As I made progress in my research, I would occasionally turn to her for advice. However, I had grown not only increasingly confident, but also increasingly convinced that it was up to me to delve into my family history. I couldn't but acknowledge her expertise and was always grateful for her help, but I couldn't work out who or what she was warning me against.

It was the curators at the Louvre. They had read Michel's memoir, and so knew of the existence of the notebooks. When I put in the claim for the Tiepolo drawing, they demanded to see the actual notebook in which it is described as "missing," as proof that the drawing was no longer in Jules's collection at the end of the war. The notebooks had become the currency for a deal.

Slowly it began to dawn on me that perhaps the museum, which had been holding onto the drawing for over seventy years, had no intention of returning the work. It was clear from documents in the Louvre archives that the museum had known for a long time that Jules had owned it before the war. Perhaps the museum was hoping to find inconsistences and contradictions in the notebook that might put my claim in doubt.

I had an instinctive feeling that they much preferred to hold on to the shepherd.

It was agony having to follow Elizabeth's advice. I couldn't bear not being able to show Jules's notebooks to people, not being able to share them. I'd have loved to publish them, to donate copies to art libraries so that anybody could consult them. I wanted students to consult them and researchers to analyze them. Above all I wanted to be able to say: *Look, see what an amazing man, what a marvelous collector Jules Strauss was! A collector who loved his paintings and their histories so much that he never stopped trying to find out more about them. An art lover who thought that selling and buying art was less important than having an exhaustive, intimate knowledge of a work.*

"An artist leaves behind a body of work, through which his memory survives. But a collector? What remains of Jules Strauss's legacy?" wondered Hélène Demoriane back in 1961. It's a good question. What does remain of my great-grandfather, the erudite collector, the man on an endless mission to find out more?

After months of research, just as I was beginning to commit my family's story to paper, I began to wonder. What right did I have to write about people I had never known? Was I betraying the truth, getting things wrong in my confusion?

Every time I felt like this, I would open Jules's notebook and see the words: "*Errare humanum est!* But I plead good faith." Once again, Jules was my guide.

XXV

JULES'S SIGNATURE

October 2019. It was the first day of the historic Leonardo da Vinci exhibition marking the five hundredth anniversary of the artist's death, and a huge crowd was gathered beneath the great glass pyramid in the main courtyard of the Louvre. I had in my pocket the list of the sixty frames my great-grandfather had donated to the museum that I had finally come to see. I decided to start with the great Italian painters: Leonardo, Titian, Raphael, Veronese.

Inside the office of the Society of the Friends of the Louvre was a long line of people hoping to snag tickets for the show. On one wall hung the exhibition poster featuring *Portrait of an Unknown Woman,* one of the paintings on my list. Tens of thousands of visitors from all over the world were going to admire this masterpiece, in a frame that Jules had picked out—a fact that I was probably the only person to know.

I hadn't looked in detail at the list of frames, simply stuffed it into a drawer, until one day a perceptive publisher pointed out to me that the frames were not inconsequential: "They aren't just a way of displaying paintings, they're the living trace of Jules, a way for him to continue to exist in the present. The frames are his signature," the publisher said. The way he said it sent a shiver down my spine. I'd never thought of it like that.

I pushed my way through the crowd of visitors. I thought of Jules crossing these very galleries on days when the museum was closed, the framer Lebrun following on his heels. I thought of Marie-Louise bringing Michel here as a child. Unlike me, they, too, must have felt a little bit at home here, whereas I rarely come anymore. I can't bear the noise and the crowds, and I always feel a little lost, barely even capable of following the sign pointing toward the *Mona Lisa*.

A few hundred steps and visitors farther on, I came to the Grand Gallery and the painters of the Italian Renaissance: biblical scenes, portraits of the Virgin Mary, multiple depictions of the Madonna and child, religious paintings on New Testament themes. The first frame on the list was that of Raphael's *Saint Michael Vanquishing Satan*, depicting the struggle of man against himself and his demons, a theme that felt all too familiar to me.

There was a small label alongside each painting. I looked to see if there was any mention of Jules Strauss, but his name was nowhere to be found.

There was another Raphael on the list, *Virgin and Child with Saint John the Baptist*, but I couldn't see it anywhere. I asked one of the museum guards, who told me it was a bit farther along on the right. I still couldn't find it. When I went back and asked the guard again, her colleague pointed at a small sign: "This work has been temporarily removed for restoration."

In spite of myself, I found myself blurting out, "My great-grandfather donated the frame!"

I had to say it, precisely because it wasn't written any-where—I had to say it for him, and for me, as a way of standing out from the crowd, so that some trace of his mem-ory remained. Unsurprisingly, the guards appeared entirely unimpressed. Fortunately, I stopped there. I didn't go on about the number of frames he had donated.

A little farther on, in the corridor off to the right leading to the gallery housing the *Mona Lisa*, a long queue of people with their cellphones waited patiently to take a selfie with the most famous painting in the world. The security measures were impressive, the painting protected by a thick casing of bulletproof glass. I remembered the story of its theft a cen-tury earlier and wondered idly if it would be possible to steal the *Mona Lisa* today.

The *Mona Lisa* was not looking out from a frame donated by Jules, but he had donated the frame of a por-trait on the opposite wall that I love, Titian's *Man with a Glove*, a young man who looks both sorrowful and dis-enchanted. He is well-dressed but slightly unkempt, and sports the faintest shadow of a beard, as though it were the morning after a party. I'd sometimes used the painting as inspiration for a writing exercise for my students, to write an interior monologue. Obviously then I had no idea of the story behind its frame.

I was still groping for the intention behind Jules's gift. Had he chosen paintings he particularly liked, or was it simply that he had found some frames with the right dimensions? Was it pure philanthropy, given that his bequest is nowhere mentioned, or just an amusing game with nothing more at stake than aesthetics?

As I was leaving the gallery one of the museum guards stopped me.

"What did you say your grandfather's name was?" she asked.

"Jules Strauss."

She stared at me. "That's incredible."

I waited for her to tell me something extraordinary, some new secret.

"Jules Strauss was my grandfather!" I stared at her, dumbstruck. She repeated herself. "Yes, he was my grandfather too!"

Then she glanced back at her two colleagues and burst out laughing.

I felt such a fool. How ridiculous to have told the first guard I came across that my forebear had donated the frames. How pathetic to be bragging, seventy years after the fact, to a total stranger, about someone whose name was completely unknown to them.

I had never seen such crowds as there were for the Leonardo show in my life. It was impossible to get near the paintings and I had to snake my way past other visitors to peer at *The*

Virgin of the Rocks, with its massive, nearly seven-foot-high frame. I could see no trace whatsoever of where Lebrun had shaved the wood to adjust it to the dimensions of the canvas.

I turned away, wearily, and searched for the exit. I decided not to look at any more frames today. I'd come back another day with my children. Maybe I'd make it into a game for them: "See how many of your great-great-grandfather's frames you can find."

In a month, a year, a century even, these frames will still be here. They will continue to display the masterpieces that millions of people will admire long after Jules Strauss's name has ceased to mean anything to anyone. People will continue to be dazzled by Raphael and Titian's portraits, Veronese's Virgin Mary. Perhaps very occasionally some erudite art lover or art history student will pause for a moment in front of the gilded wooden foliage that surrounds Raphael's *Portrait of Baldassare Castiglione* and remember the name of the discreet donor who determined in 1935 that a "beautiful painting deserves a beautiful frame." The thought that my great-grandfather is immortalized by these frames makes me ridiculously happy.

As I was leaving the Grand Gallery, I recalled a photograph taken here during the war, of hundreds of empty frames piled up on the floor, filling the corridors of the museum. The paintings themselves had been sent away from Paris for safekeeping, on the initiative of Jacques Jaujard, the then director of the museum. Among them was the *Mona Lisa*, hidden in a château in southwest France. The works were transported by night, in secret, in trucks so tall sometimes they could barely squeeze beneath the bridges they passed. Throughout the museum's rescue operation and the exodus of its masterpieces, Jules's frames must have remained here, propped up against the walls along with thousands of others, awaiting better days.

XXVI

JEWISH, ME?

It was becoming clear to me as I followed Jules's trail that I had been avoiding talking about the fact that he was Jewish. For most of my life the question of Judaism had not concerned me at all. But for several months, since I'd begun looking into a history I'd known nothing about, I found myself wondering how and why we as a family had almost entirely erased that part of our identity. I felt something remained, however faint a trace, and I began to try to detect and identify what I had until then refused to consider, perhaps out of some odd sense of loyalty.

Things had never been straightforward in my family. My paternal great-grandparents and grandparents were Jewish. My father claimed to have had an epiphany at the age of eighteen which led to his conversion to Catholicism in 1940, along with two of his first cousins. My mother always claimed that it was not for fear of the Nazis but because of a genuine religious conviction. Although he eventually grew to consider himself, like his hero Montaigne, an agnostic, he was buried according to Catholic rites. His cousin Jacques remained an ardent Catholic until the end of his life.

I was baptized Catholic, as were my mother and husband. I received my first communion, my confirmation, and made my declaration of faith. And then—I married my first husband, a nonpracticing Jew, in a civil ceremony. Ah yes, how endlessly complicated these things are. We decided that our son, Élie, would be neither circumcised nor baptized.

After our divorce, I married Henri, a practicing Catholic, this time in a church. We chose to have our daughters baptized. Henri likes to take the girls to Mass on Sundays, something I was finding increasingly difficult, despite having committed to bringing them up religious. All this research into my family history was throwing everything into question. I was beginning to wonder about my Jewish roots, trying to work out if anything of that heritage remains in me.

I knew Jules was Jewish, but I had no idea what that meant in practice. According to my aunt Nadine, the family never celebrated the Jewish festivals. When I asked about her religious education, she told me that at the age of twelve, she was invited to a bar mitzvah celebration in a grand hotel, where she asked a waiter for a ham sandwich. "You have to understand, we didn't feel Jewish in the slightest, we had no idea what it meant," she said, half amused, half amazed. At the time I didn't doubt the truth of her anecdote, and I don't think she did either. But now I'm not so sure. I think Nadine knew very well by the time she was twelve that Jews don't eat pork, especially at bar mitzvah parties. I rather suspect that because she understood that the family was not like other Jewish families, either unconsciously or by provocation and a kind of loyalty, she asked for ham to show she wasn't like the other children there. Perhaps she wanted to emulate her parents' and grandparents' efforts to erase their Jewish identity. This anecdote is a painful reminder of the paradox of a family forced by war to assume their Jewish identity which, for reasons I didn't quite understand, they had always refused to acknowledge.

Marie-Hélène told me her uncle Roger, a decorated former army officer, detested "all that Jewish stuff." He never wanted to hear a word about it. Yet he was deported from France and murdered at Auschwitz, precisely because he was Jewish. I could understand why his son Claude had rejected this identity, which had never brought anything but tragedy into his life.

What did being Jewish mean for these children whose parents were almost entirely nonpracticing? Did they follow any Jewish practice or ever set foot inside a synagogue?

In Jules and Marie-Louise's lifetimes, and the lifetimes of their children, too, bourgeois Jews tended to marry Jews from the same milieu. Their weddings took place in a synagogue as a matter of course. Françoise, Élisabeth, and André all married in Paris's Great Synagogue on rue de la Victoire. All had Jewish spouses: Roger Sorbac, Louis Baer, and Aline de Gunzbourg respectively. But in the generation that came after, it became increasingly common in their milieu for Jews to marry out. Not one of Jules and Marie-Louise's grandsons married a Jewish woman. Aunt Nadine didn't marry at all. For this family, it was the end of the matrilineal transmission of Jewish identity.

I'd heard people talk about assimilated Jews, but I didn't really know what that meant. Assimilated to what, to whom? To non-Jews? To Catholics, to nonbelievers? What I did know is that if I had been born in 1940 to a Catholic mother and a Jewish father, I would have been considered Jewish according to the racial laws—albeit a Jew who knew nothing whatsoever about Jewish religion or culture, who had never even lit the Sabbath candles.

I tried to imagine how my assimilated, nonpracticing family must have reacted in the face of mounting anti-Semitism and anti-Jewish laws. Did they realize that however insignificant their attachment to Judaism, they were unequivocally deemed to be Jews in the eyes of the Nazis? Was Roger Sorbac the human manifestation of obliviousness in the face of danger? Had he, like so many others half a century after the Dreyfus Affair, believed himself protected by the medals he had been awarded as an officer during the First World War?

Nadine showed me Jules's and Marie-Louise's baptism certificates that had been gathering dust in a drawer. She had completely forgotten that her grandparents were baptized in 1942, as was quite common among the Parisian Jewish bourgeoisie during the Occupation, in a usually vain attempt to avoid persecution.

My ex-husband had also begun exploring his Jewish roots. One morning in September 2018, he sent me an email telling me he'd done an online DNA test. The results had come back informing him he was 48 percent Ashkenazi Jewish.

The rest a mixture of English and Spanish. But can being Jewish really be reduced to a DNA analysis?

Wondering how all these disparate elements forge an individual's identity, I decided to speak to a childhood friend with a similar family history to mine. Agathe David-Weill is the scion of a large banking family of Alsatian Jews on her father's side. On her mother's side she is Catholic. I asked her if she felt in any way Jewish.

"No, not at all, except when I think about the war, and then I realize that I'd have been categorized as Jewish in any case." I was interested in this, since my father converted to Catholicism during the war, and her father just after. Both men insisted that it was a question of belief, but I found it rather strange. "My father was brought up with a real Jewish culture," she told me. "Jokes, a smattering of Yiddish, but no religion whatsoever. His big joke was that people would wish him a happy new year when it was the Jewish new year, and he'd pretend he thought they were crazy. I think his whole family had done everything they could to assimilate and erase any trace of otherness. It was a strange mixture of pride and ignorance."

I didn't find her father's joke funny. It reminded me of Nadine and her ham sandwich.

Several days later, my son Élie returned home from celebrating Rosh Hashana with his paternal grandfather, and for the first time in my life I proudly wished him a happy new year. Though I didn't yet dare utter the words *shana tova*, at that moment I had the uncanny sense of being reconciled with myself.

Back in the mid-1980s, my elder brother, Julien, began investigating the Baer family's Alsatian roots. He discovered that one of our ancestors was a rabbi called Lazare Lazarius. Even today Julien regularly sends me his favorite quotations from Rebbe Nachman of Breslov: "There is no despair in the world, at all"; "It's a great mitzvah—a religious duty—to always be happy." There was another maxim Julien liked to quote that I took particularly to heart: "Never ask directions from someone who knows where you are going, because you might not get lost. "

One day, amid all this contemplation about my family's relationship to Judaism, I spotted a poster in the window of a local store advertising an open-air screening of Louis Malle's 1987 movie *Au Revoir les Enfants* in Suresnes, a suburb of Paris, at the site of the notorious prison of Mont-Valérien, where over a thousand resistants were executed during the Second World War. It all came rushing back to me—when my father was sixty, though he had never acted before, he was given a part in a brief but memorable scene. The movie is set during the Occupation, and the scene takes place in a provincial restaurant. Julien Quentin, a student at a Carmelite boarding school in the French countryside, has been taken out to lunch by his mother, with his older brother and a Jewish friend, Jean Kippelstein, who attends the same school under a false name. All of a sudden, my father's character, an elegant, older gentleman dining alone, is disturbed by men from the Milice, the paramilitary force of the collaborationist Vichy regime, who demand to see his papers. Julien's brother protests, but no one tries to stop the men, and my father's character is ordered to leave. I can still see the sorrow and humiliation etched on his face.

I remember my father regaling us with stories, how they shot the scene dozens of times, and he had to light his cigarette at the beginning of each take. He was sweetly proud of having managed to change his one line of dialogue: "The rabbit stew was reasonable" didn't seem quite right to him, so he changed it to, "The rabbit stew was not bad at all." It was very important to him to find just the right phrase, the one best suited to the correct use of the French language, which he held in the utmost esteem. But he didn't say anything about the character he played, or the memories the scene must have stirred in him.

It was a poignant irony of history to find himself at the age of sixty, playing a character being punished for being a Jew in a scene that might have been lifted from an episode in his own grandfather's life. He, like his grandfather, had been a victim of the Vichy anti-Jewish laws, even though he barely considered himself Jewish. Is it possible to entirely escape one's origins?

Instead of casting a professional actor, Louis Malle asked my father, an old friend, to take the part. Looking at the pictures from the shoot, I can see why. The character my father played was rather like him—anxious, dignified, gentle, and discreet. When I try to conjure his face, I picture a still from the movie. A close-up of his face in profile, his swept back hair, almost entirely white with a few coppery glints. A prominent, aquiline nose and a narrow white moustache grazing his upper lip, like Clark Gable. The way he had of holding his hand up to his mouth and lowering his eyes with a polite smile.

His melancholy expression on screen is that of a man who knows his role too well. Watching the movie, I had the feeling he wasn't playing a part at all, that this man—who had fled France, escaped deportation, abandoned religion— inhabited the role as if it had really happened to him.

My cousin Marie-Hélène sent me a document. It appeared to be Jules's will:

> On this day, 14th April 1942, I, Jules Strauss, of sound mind and body, request to be buried in a private civil ceremony, with the greatest simplicity. I wish to be cremated, and for my ashes to be thrown into a common grave.

I couldn't understand this request at all. I called Marie-Hélène and we spoke for a long time. We both felt such grief and sorrow at the sheer despair Jules must have felt as he penned these lines the year before he died. We didn't dare try to interpret it. Neither of us felt we had the right to put ourselves in his shoes.

What was the symbolism of this final request? I could understand that Jules hadn't wanted to be buried according to rites that he didn't follow, but why this bizarre detail about his ashes? Marie-Hélène linked it to the fate of the murdered Jews of Europe, conjuring images of concentration camps, crematoria, bodies piled up in mass graves.

So many questions I had never asked. I knew the family had been separated during the war, that the grandsons had joined the Free French Forces, that only Jules and Marie-Louise had remained in Paris. Who had attended Jules's funeral in July 1943? Had his wishes been respected? This time, I decided not to ask Nadine.

XXVII

AN APPOINTMENT AT THE MINISTRY OF CULTURE

March 2017. It was very warm for early spring. Lunch with my friend Denis in the Palais-Royal gardens was not as relaxing as I'd hoped. I found myself unable to talk about anything other than my anxiety and impatience for the hoped-for return of the Tiepolo drawing. There would be a lot at stake during the afternoon's meeting at the Ministry of Culture in the imposing building that surrounded the gardens, and I felt considerably more apprehensive than honored by the invitation.

I entered the building and paused at the foot of the grand staircase, seized by a disagreeable sensation, the fear that I was about to let myself be impressed by this official occasion. I couldn't bear the thought that some misplaced sense of pride and gratitude might make me forget the indignation that had brought me here. I was not at all sure I had the confidence to speak up and insist on what I believed was right.

A young woman led us down several long corridors and showed us into an opulent wood-paneled room. I walked over to the window to admire the view over the gardens. I thought of Colette and Cocteau, who had both once lived there. I wondered which were their windows. Neither of them would have had to worry about their belongings being expropriated.

The Ministry of Culture had organized a meeting with the minister's principal private secretary and the signatories, of which I was one, of a letter requesting the establishment of a research unit within the MNR, the organization that deals with the repository of works of art recovered after the war held in French museums until they can be returned to the descendants of their rightful owners. Two thousand of these works are still held in French museums. A temporary repository whose existence is repeatedly prolonged.

Feeling very intimidated, I was the last to take my place at the long rectangular table, at which point I realized with horror that I was sitting on the wrong side, with ministry employees. All the other signatories were sitting on the opposite side of the table. Flustered, I discreetly tried to shift my chair enough so that I was sitting across from the private secretary. I found myself neither on one side nor the other, overcome by a ridiculous feeling of discomfort.

But I had no reason to feel this way. I was an "interested party," fighting to recover a drawing held in the Louvre that rightfully belonged to my family. I kept reminding myself I had something to say as I glanced at the civil servant to my left, whose eyes were glued to his cellphone and who proceeded to spend the entire meeting sending text messages.

The meeting began with a lengthy, carefully worded presentation explaining how the topic would be addressed. We must have spent at least half an hour failing to get to the point of why we were there.

Everyone was given the chance to speak. A poised lawyer with an unwavering smile talked articulately and clearly, but afterward I couldn't remember a word of what she'd said. Emmanuelle Polack, strangely confident and calm, spoke of the necessity of instructing future museum curators about the issue of spoliation. Several important questions were raised: Would it be better to withdraw the MNR from the aegis of the National Museums? Should the works instead be placed in Paris's Museum of Jewish Art and History? Did this risk marginalizing the issue and turning it into something that concerned only Jews?

Whether it was the heat, or the gilded glories of the Republic, the atmosphere of the meeting seemed sluggish rather than urgent. When were we going to address the only thing that actually mattered: the return of the two thousand works to their rightful owners? We needed to be efficient. When someone at the other end of the table mentioned figures, I heard myself cry out, in spite of myself, "Just five per cent of these looted artworks have been returned to their owners in seventy-five years!"

The head of the CIVS, the Commission for the Compensation of Victims of Spoliation, was seated directly opposite the private secretary, clearly better to draw attention to his status. He was a man of late middle age, who came across as supercilious and bullish. It was hard to believe the words of a man under whose direction there had been so few restitutions—fewer than twenty in the last twenty years.

To hear him tell it, his organization, with its branches in Germany, was vast and all-powerful. If this were indeed the case, it was unclear why there had been so few positive outcomes. This must be why I still couldn't bring myself to fill in the compensation claim forms on behalf of my own family. Now that I knew all about my grandmother's unsuccessful attempts, I was determined to keep hold of this dossier and do all the necessary research myself.

The descendant of a well-known collector stressed the importance of cross-referencing family archives. It was beginning to feel as though everyone was trying to find themselves a place within some hypothetical future organization. I really wanted to be appointed spokesperson for the families, but I wasn't sure if I had the authority, or if I had what it took to listen, advise, help other people.

At the same time, I was painfully aware how absurd it was to be thinking like this, when what mattered was gaining justice for all the families. I felt petty. I wanted to take part in the discussion but didn't know what to say. I had come ill-prepared, apparently believing that the mere fact of being the descendant of a victim of spoliation sanctioned me to speak off the top of my head. Instead of listening to the others, I was desperately trying to think of something intelligent to say. If nothing else, I owed it to my family, who had been silenced for decades.

So I raised my hand and began to speak. "When I found the Tiepolo drawing on the Ministry of Culture's looted art website, the text alongside was extremely detailed, and included the name of its owner, Monsieur Strauss. In case there were any doubts about the owner, all I needed to do was to cross-check it with auction records, which show that the buyer of this drawing in 1928 was 'Jules Strauss, living at 60 Avenue du Bois' (now Avenue Foch). Simply doing a quick online search for 'Strauss' would have brought up the name Michel Strauss. It would have been very easy to find this Monsieur Strauss and discuss the drawing with him. Yet no one ever did."

I brought up a pastel drawing by Adélaïde Labille-Guiard, stolen by the Nazis from the Gunzbourg family. "It's quite evident from the Ministry of Culture's own website that the drawing was stolen from Michel's maternal grandfather, Pierre de Gunzbourg—so why has it still not been returned to the family? There are probably other pictures that could be returned, but perhaps the Ministry of Culture does not have the means to deal with its own dossiers, in other words to undertake the search for descendants of the original owners, once they've been identified." Several sympathetic faces around the table were turned toward me, and the private secretary nodded her enthusiastic agreement.

It was time to draw the meeting to a close. With admirable skill, the private secretary summed things up at great length, with much roundabout formulation, affirming every potential outcome without rubbing anyone the wrong way. Most of all, she managed to offer us hope, without any real commitment.

I let myself be taken in, and after ten minutes of her nimble rhetoric, was convinced the ministry was going to act. Either to create a working group, or to give the go-ahead to the CIVS to do so. I stood up and warmly thanked the private secretary.

When I left the ministry the Louvre pyramid was gleaming in the afternoon sunshine. I thought about Jules's name carved into the donors' wall, and Tiepolo's drawing, sleeping in the museum's reserves. I remembered Jules's correspondence with Germain Bazin about the donation of the sixty frames. And then the look of the head of the CIVS as he explained why no effort had been made to return the drawing to us: "There were so many Strausses at the time, how could we have known which one it was?" I could barely believe the ingratitude and the injustice.

As I crossed the Carrousel bridge that spanned the Seine, the sun was going down and at last the heat of the day was abating. My feeling of optimism had faded. What had the woman from the ministry really said? After seventy-five years was it possible to believe that anything was going to change now? Even if the Louvre did return Jules's drawing, would the other families be so lucky?

XXVIII

RESTITUTION

> *"I believe that the restitution of looted property to the Jews is an undertaking of justice and humanity whose moral and political significance far surpasses the material value of the items involved. It needs to be, in the eyes of both France and the world, one of the foremost tangible manifestations of the re-establishment of law and republican legitimacy,"* Professor Terroine, administrator–receiver of the Lyons Jewish Affairs Commission, December 29, 1944.

Henri and I went to visit Nadine to ask her who had written the word "missing" in the margin of Jules's notebook. Because Nadine writes with difficulty now, Henri penned on her behalf: "I confirm that the word 'missing' is in the handwriting of my grandmother Marie-Louise Strauss." Then she signed in her shaky hand. Without this document, we would never have been able to recover the drawing.

And so, over a year after it had first appeared on my computer screen, Tiepolo's *Shepherd* was at last to be returned to the descendants of Jules Strauss by the Minister of Culture.

April 2017. I curled my hair and put on a pretty dress. I decided to walk over the Pont des Arts to the Ministry of Culture on my own. I needed to prepare myself mentally for the event. My heart was pounding. I was afraid my words wouldn't be equal to the occasion. Moreover, it didn't seem right that it was I who was to speak on behalf of the family, given that Jules's grandchildren, who had actually known him, were going to be there.

What I found most remarkable about the occasion was the thought of seeing them together, for the first time in many years. Nadine and Michel were both old. This might be the last time they saw each other. It was the memory of Jules that had brought us all together. Ancestral love has the strange and marvelous power of uniting people who have little else in common.

My father had been dead for twenty years, yet I couldn't stop thinking about him. Was it for him, the memory of his silences, his moments of absence, that I had thrown myself into this adventure? I hope he would have been proud of me that day.

Nadine was waiting for me in front of the ministry, leaning unsteadily upon her cane. Would she be able to manage walking through the grand reception rooms? Seeing Emmanuelle Polack standing just behind her, a warm smile on her face, filled me with confidence. Just as I arrived, Henri rode up on his bicycle, accompanied by our two little girls in their best dresses. My heart leaped. This was not a time for doubt, it was time for celebration.

I took Nadine's arm. I wanted her to be the first person to enter the ornate salon where the ceremony was to take place.

A friend filmed Nadine as she walked slowly across the room to see the drawing. She looked at it and said only that she thought it was nothing special, that it was rather discolored and small. But she stood in silence for a long time before the portrait of Jules that had been blown up for the occasion and was displayed alongside the shepherd.

The modesty and grace, and the fine features of both men, slowly grew on me. I stood in silence next to Nadine, both of us deeply moved.

In my head, a debate was raging. One voice claimed it was a hollow victory. "Do you really think there's any meaning to this, seventy-five years after Jules's death? Who do you think you are? Don't you think there are other ways to make yourself useful?" The other was more temperate, speaking of justice, reparation, homage.

The room was filling up with cousins I had never met, curators who seemed less than thrilled at the return of the drawing and who avoided greeting me, and some of the archivists who had helped with my research, who came up to thank me for inviting them. Michel had come over from London with his wife, Sally. Claude had written to apologize that he wouldn't be able to make the journey from his home in Argentina, he was too old, but I suspected that everything that reminded him of that time in his life was too hard for him to bear. His brother Jacques was there with his daughters.

People were crowding around me, plying me with questions. Some were simply curious: "Are there more paintings to be recovered? How did you find it all?" I'd been warned not to reveal everything to the curators, whose questions were more pointed. "Have you had the drawing valued? What will you do with it? Are you planning to sell?"

It is not uncommon for curators to criticize Jewish families who sell their inherited works, accusing them of caring only about the money—the ultimate anti-Semitic slur—but what are families supposed to do when several descendants find themselves joint owners of a valuable work of art?

A few people were clearly suspicious of my motives. One of my cousins confronted me angrily: "How come I never heard any of these stories of looted art?" I didn't know how to respond. Luckily, just at that moment, the minister of culture, Audrey Azoulay, began to speak. I found the situation, this overlap of generations and periods of history, so unnerving and strange that I struggled to concentrate.

She began by acknowledging how "absurd it is that the drawing had been held in the Louvre for over seventy years, its owner unknown—the very museum that had received generous donations from Strauss himself, a museum he knew well, and which knew him well, too, for not only was he a benefactor but also a long-standing and eminent member of the Society of the Friends of the Louvre."

She went on, "A knowledgeable connoisseur, Strauss was the link between art historians, curators, and collectors throughout Europe [...] His passion for art, his generosity,

and his erudition collided with the inhumane Nazis machine
[. . .] Strauss experienced persecution, the wearing of the
yellow star, and the arrest of his son-in-law Roger, father
of Claude and Jacques, deported on the first convoy out
of France in March 1942, and murdered at Auschwitz.
Jules himself died at the age of eighty-two in the suicide
of Europe."

It hadn't occurred to me she would take the opportu-
nity to pay homage to other members of the family. "When
the war began, his four grandchildren were all under twenty.
Claude Sorbac joined the Second Armored Division and
remained with it from Normandy all the way to Germany.
Jacques Sorbac was a French commando under Henri d'Astier
de La Vigerie. Nadine Baer worked as an interpreter in the
Women's Voluntary Division of the Free French Forces.
And Philippe Baer, who is no longer with us, was also in the
Second Armored Division. What a lesson for us all!"

I was totally unprepared for this mention of my father.
I could hardly breathe. I didn't dare catch the eye of my
mother or my brother Édouard. I glanced instead at my son,
Élie, who had never met his grandfather. A question flashed
through my mind: "What was I up to when I was twenty?"

Azoulay continued to address Jules's grandchildren. "You
knew Jules and Marie-Louise Strauss, their apartment on
Avenue Foch, their passion for art; you are the link between
that era and today, this building on rue de Valois, and the
return of this drawing after seven decades." Then she turned
to address the next generation. "Your family has maintained

its links with the art world. Jules Strauss's great-grandchildren are now following in his footsteps, faithful to this remarkable tradition, in spite of—or perhaps because of—this history."

A sentence from the dismissive 1961 article in *Connaissance des Arts* flashed through my mind: "What remains of Jules Strauss's legacy?" A week or two after the ceremony the same magazine published a brief, congratulatory article: "On April 13 2017, Audrey Azoulay, Minister of Culture and Communication, formally returned a drawing attributed to the Italian artist Giovanni Battista Tiepolo to the descendants of its owners, the banker Jules Strauss and his wife Marie-Louise, whose art collection was confiscated by the Nazis in 1941 and 1942." Something of Jules's legacy did remain after all, and this made me very happy.

Afterward, a strikingly good-looking woman came up to me. She was a celebrated art historian, and author of a well-known book on looted art. "The work of a historian is a plea for love," she said.

I'd spent a long time thinking about what I was going to say that day. Eventually I realized that I needed to speak with the utmost sincerity, to admit, however naïve it sounded, that this quest had been the most fascinating and important thing I had ever done in my life. As I gave my speech on behalf of the family, I looked up and caught first Henri's eye, then Édouard's. I was very moved. My brother looked completely caught off guard by his emotions.

After the ceremony was over, deeply relieved, I mused to myself that I'd pulled it off. After this I could be sure of myself. I had to remember this feeling, stop constantly doubting myself. I felt my entire being flood with joy.

Nonetheless, after I bade farewell to everybody and left the building, a somber thought occurred to me. In the absence of my brother Julien, the whole occasion seemed, in a way, pointless. I'd spoken to him about every new discovery, kept him abreast of the tiniest details, not to mention all my doubts and uncertainties. He encouraged and supported me, and kept me levelheaded. Every time we spoke, he'd repeat, "Don't forget, you're not doing this for the family, you're doing it for yourself. Don't expect compliments or gratitude."

But he hadn't been there. I'd discovered a drawing that no one had even known existed, but I'd failed to bring together all the people I loved, or to make them happy.

I wanted to keep the Tiepolo at home for a little while, but Andrew, ever prudent, insisted it be stored in a safe at Sotheby's. I didn't argue, though I would have loved to have spent a little more time in the company of Jules's shepherd.

XXIX

HOMESICK

In July 2019, five years after the unexpected encounter with Andrew that had triggered my deep dive into my family history, we took a vacation to the birthplace of Caetano Veloso. We were on the beach one morning when I heard the news of the death of another great Brazilian musician, João Gilberto, most famous for *Chega de Saudade*, "No More Blues." For no apparent reason, I was overwhelmed with a great wave of melancholy. Henri and the children were playing in the waves. I went to shelter behind a café so I could call Nadine, who was stuck in Paris on her own all summer. A little while after the ceremony for the return of the drawing she'd broken her hip and now she couldn't leave her apartment. I still wasn't sure if I had done the right thing stirring up her memories. Perhaps she would have been better off holding on to her happy childhood nostalgia and letting go of the rest.

I looked for a patch of shade beneath the trees, up against the cliffs bordered with coconut palms and tall, swaying trees whose name I didn't know. I sat cross-legged on the sand, trying to intuit Jules's presence in the breeze. I wanted to know if it was time to leave him in peace and move on to something else.

"I haven't finished my book yet!" I said out loud.

"And? You can write about the past without living in the past, can you not?" I heard Jules's response as if he were there beside me.

"How can I find out who you were without getting close to you?"

"It's an illusion. You will never know who I was."

Back at the hotel I spent most of the day lying in a hammock, in the shadow of the cliffs that loomed over the ocean. I was worried I was spoiling everyone's holiday. I didn't surf. I didn't play with my daughters. All I did was slather them in sunscreen, nag them about staying in the shade in the heat of the day, and worry about what time we should eat. I knew none of that made me a good mother. I was preoccupied. I was seven thousand kilometers away from the archives, and I felt stupidly homesick.

Occasionally I would leave the shade of the beach umbrella and chat politely with other French holidaymakers. Carole, on holiday with her children, was reading a novel by Olivier Guez about Josef Mengele. Mengele, known as the Angel of Death, was an SS officer and physician who performed horrific experiments on prisoners at Auschwitz. After the war he escaped to Argentina and then Brazil, where he died in 1979. One day we ended up debating whether his son, Rolf, should have denounced his father when he found out he was living in Brazil under a false identity. According to him, his father had no regrets about what he had done. Rolf met his father just twice in his life and changed his surname. Shouldn't he have had him arrested? Or must one protect one's parents at any cost? When a journalist asked him why he hadn't alerted the police, he replied:

"I couldn't. He was a monster, but he was my father."

I wondered idly if one of the houses on the cliff top might be sheltering some other old Nazi still on the run.

I was reading about another search for roots, *The Art of Losing*, by Alice Zeniter, but I was finding it hard to get into. I was too immersed in my own quest, a thousand leagues from Zeniter's Algeria. I did detect one thing in common though: the silence of later generations, and the difficulty of exploring a history that we knew only by its absence. "When you're reduced to searching Wikipedia for information about the country you're supposedly from, then maybe there's a problem," writes Zeniter.

I'd managed to dig up a few places and dates, and I already knew the names, but other than that, what had I found out?

The sun was burning hot. I went up to my room to listen to Elizabeth Royer on the radio. There had, at last, been a proposal to set up a commission to return the twelve hundred remaining works of art in the MNR, which were still, like the Tiepolo, held in various French museums. Elizabeth was wary of "yet another commission." It was the extract from Modiano's novel *Dora Bruder*, chosen as an epigraph to the report, that made her wary:

"Traces remain in registers, and we don't know where they are hidden, or who is safeguarding them, or if they will agree to show them to you. Or perhaps the existence of the registers has simply been forgotten. We simply need a little patience."

How on earth do they expect families to continue to be patient, after more than seventy years? Nonetheless, unlike Elizabeth, I still had a bit of faith, and I hoped I might help other families.

One evening, all squashed up together on the bed in our little Brazilian bungalow, we watched the Pixar movie *Coco*, set in Mexico on the Day of the Dead, when families decorate an altar in honor of their ancestors. If they forget to do this, the dead vanish completely, in a kind of double bereavement. One haunting scene had us all in tears: the little boy hums a song in his grandmother Coco's ear, the same song her father had sung to her when she was a child, almost a hundred years before. Coco is my daughter's nickname. The elderly woman's face lights up as she remembers the tune, and she begins to sing along, *Remember me*. She hasn't forgotten her father, and so he will not disappear from the world of the dead. She puts his photo back on the altar, so that he can come back to see her, once a year, on the *Día de los Muertos*.

If only these two worlds could really coexist, if only our forebears could remain as close to us as they are in this children's animation. How I wanted to be able to celebrate them too.

XXX

"WHEN YOU CLOSE YOUR EYES"

The real estate agent's cruel euphemism left me speechless. He actually stood in front of Nadine, who had no choice but to sell her apartment under a French system that is similar to that involving a reverse mortgage in the United States, and deployed his carefully chosen words. Though their implication horrified me, I couldn't help smiling at the image of the lengthy training sessions that agents must undergo on "How to talk to aged clients about their imminent demise." I wished I could help Nadine, so she wouldn't have to give up ownership of her apartment and speculate on her own death.

The previous evening Henri had asked me why I was so resistant to the idea of the apartment being sold. It was the family apartment, which my father had half owned, and he in turn had left his share to my brothers and me when he died. I was shocked at Henri's question and burst into tears when he suggested that perhaps I felt I was being denied my inheritance. A material inheritance, yes, but also a symbolic one, for the apartment was all I owned that had once belonged to my father.

It was a feeling I had difficulty articulating, of a symbolic "handing over" that had never taken place. Henri suggested that I was experiencing it as an "expropriation," but I found the word too strong—this was what had happened to Jules.

No, this time it was, again, a financial issue. Did I have the right to hold it against my aunt? I knew it was extremely difficult for her, too, and she didn't have any choice.

Seeking affection and reassurance, I emailed my brothers, who presumably had other things on their minds than my emotional state. Julien responded right away, saying he would quite understand if I wanted us to pull out of the sale. Though he wasn't wealthy, he was ready to renounce his share. Édouard, however, was quite annoyed: he didn't share my sentimentality when it came to property. Since he couldn't be there for the real estate agent's visit, I told him I understood, it was no problem, I'd deal with it on my own. But when I spotted his face on a poster advertising a film or play on a bus or a kiosk, I felt a tug of sadness at his absence.

Nadine had already called me three times that morning, wondering if I knew when she would receive the money from the sale. Her hearing aid was acting up and she couldn't hear me. She put the phone on speaker and there was a booming echo.

"I'm on my way to sign!" I practically yelled at her, before hanging up a little abruptly.

But for a whole week I avoided the agent and kept putting off our meeting, using the children and the start of the school year as an excuse.

My brothers and my aunt signed the sale agreement. I was the only person who hadn't. A week went by as I flailed around for an alternative solution, some clever ruse that would mean we wouldn't have to go through with it. Finally, on Friday, I phoned the agent and made an appointment to meet him at 5 p.m. at a café near my apartment. It was too early for a drink, but I ordered two glasses of champagne anyway, though I felt far from celebratory.

I accepted Monsieur M***'s offer, which was 30 percent below the market price. I had nothing against the agent. He was polite and professional and came to meet each of us at our convenience to sign the agreement. I felt a strange urge to forge a bond with him before signing, so I tried to get him to open up a bit about himself. He told me he wouldn't give up his career "for anything in the world."

"I adore lifetime annuities," he said, "plus I earn a lot more than in traditional property deals."

This was evidently the part that interested him the most. But because I am by nature empathic, I probed a little more. He explained that his clients were more interested in investing than in living in their properties, "which makes them much easier to deal with." So that was it—easy, quick, more profitable sales. Until he found himself dealing with some overemotional offspring, perhaps. I listened, somewhat skeptically. My mind wandered. A little voice inside my head kept wondering if I'd done the right thing by agreeing.

The champagne allayed my doubts, and I signed. Then,

almost lighthearted, I left and went home, relieved, in a way, to have finally made the decision.

That evening my mother called. She wanted to know why I hadn't told her we'd found a buyer. She hammered me with questions—how much had my brothers and I made, how much was my aunt going to get? Was I sure we hadn't been shortchanged?

It was partly my fault she was so insensitive. I didn't know how to explain to her how difficult the decision had been to let go of the final repository of my father and his family's memories. Realizing how upset I was, she tried to distract me with news about my actor brother.

"Did you read that adorable interview with Édouard, where he talked all about his invention of 'joyous melancholy'?"

It was indeed a charming expression, yet now that the effect of the champagne had dissipated, I found myself overwhelmed with a melancholy that was not in the least bit joyous. My father's world had gone, and there was nothing I could do. I hadn't even succeeded in gathering all his children in one place.

XXXI

MADAME DE PARABÈRE
HOLDS ON TO HER MYSTERY

She sits on a low stone wall, in a blue taffeta gown swathed in pale rose satin, its draped folds so realistic I want to reach out and touch them. She holds a split pomegranate in her left hand, while her right hand rests lightly on a pumpkin. Her lively eyes contrast with her plump cheeks. Behind her, a man looks up at a cherub, who is holding a mask in one hand.

I'd chanced upon the image online the previous year, but seeing it in real life was like discovering it for the first time. Henri and I were in the Dresden museum's storage area, where Nicolas de Largillière's masterpiece was being stored until the museum's renovations were complete. I was irritated by the staff standing too close behind me. They refused to leave Henri and me alone with the painting. So I tried to do the exercise I use in my writing workshops, when I ask my students to concentrate deeply on a painting before they begin writing, and to avoid projecting their thoughts onto it: "Gather your feelings and emotions, and write."

"We have ten minutes before we must put the picture back," said the curator.

Ten minutes. I'd been hunting for it for over a year. I had spent hours and days in different archives investigating its history, retracing its journey. Henri and I had come all the way from Paris to see it.

"Would you mind if I took a photo?"

The curator shook his head. That would not be possible. So instead, I focused my entire being on looking at Madame de Parabère, mistress of French Prince Regent Philippe II in the early eighteenth century. I wanted to delve into her very soul. I needed to understand:

"What was it that drew Jules to you? Why did he choose you?"

The canvas measured five feet high. Not being very tall, I stood almost face-to-face with the royal favorite. I addressed her, in my head:

"Don't you have a secret to tell me?"

Her expression was not remotely placid. It was confident, proud, almost too direct. Now it was she who was interrogating me:

"What are you doing here? I think you've thrown yourself into a pursuit that's too much for you. Don't you have a life? Don't you have a family?"

I heard her, but I didn't want to listen. There were so many things I wanted to know.

"Tell me all the things that have happened to you since Jules purchased you in 1928. Tell me about the first time you met! Tell me how you ended up in this museum after the war, whose hands you have passed through."

But Madame de Parabère held on to her mystery. I forced myself to engrave her image on my memory. Our ten minutes had run out. I somehow managed to retain my dignity, not to cry out, "Don't take her away so soon!" when the large metal screen to which she was attached slowly rolled her back into the stacks.

Henri put his arm around me. "The next time we see her will be in Paris, when she's returned to you. I promise." I think he, too, had spoken to Madame de Parabère. I took his hand and smiled to hide my emotion.

XXXII

"SAMMLUNG JULES STRAUSS"

December 2016. A year before our trip to Dresden.

"Nadine, have you seen this picture before?"

Brandishing a sheet of paper, I had come to question my aunt about my latest discovery.

To my utter astonishment, I had discovered on the website of the German Lost Art Foundation an eighteenth-century portrait entitled *Bildnis einer Dame als Pomona,* by Nicolas de Largillière. I barely knew any German, so I quickly scrolled down the page until I got to the words *"Provenienz: Marquis de Chaponay,"* then *"Sammlung Jules Strauss."* Henri, who had studied German at school, was able to translate the crucial word: "Collection Jules Strauss." This meant Jules was its last recorded owner, in 1938. The painting had been discovered in 1953 in the basement of the East German Finance Ministry. Between these two dates—nothing.

Nadine, no longer remotely surprised to see me turning up at odd hours, stared at length at the picture I had printed out.

"It's such a poor-quality image. The painting is considered to be Largillière's masterpiece. Did you know Madame de Parabère was the prince regent's mistress?" she said. I couldn't quite believe my ears.

"So you do recognize the painting!" I asked excitedly.

"I do not, I'm afraid."

"You're sure you never saw it on the wall in Avenue Foch when you were a child?"

"Bon Papa had so many pictures, you know. There were dozens leaning against the wall in his study. He used to hide them from Mémé, your great-grandmother."

"But how come you remember the title of the portrait?"

"Because you told me when you got here," she said tartly. "I'm not completely gaga yet, you know!"

I could swear I hadn't said anything when I arrived, but her conviction made me doubt myself. I didn't insist. I hoped that if I let her look at it for a few more minutes, some faint memory might surface.

She looked at it thoughtfully, then said briskly, "I think it's terribly dull."

Ever since I'd begun this investigation, Nadine had taken great pleasure in telling me which of the treasures of the Strauss collection she didn't care for.

"I really dislike this genre of painting. I'd have loved to have kept one of the Renoirs: *Portrait of a Girl*, now that's a gorgeous portrait! How wonderful it would have been to have it hanging in my drawing room. All those dancers by Degas I find dreadfully boring. I adore Matisse, but Bon Papa didn't collect him. We simply didn't have the same tastes, that's all."

I knew how much Nadine enjoyed not liking certain things. For her, disparagement was a natural form of modesty, a ruse to avoid being overcome by emotion, or sinking into nostalgia. I learned to interpret it as a sign of affection.

If Nadine couldn't help me, I would have to go through Jules's notebooks. If I had been more methodical, I'd have started there. I began carefully turning the brittle pages of the first notebook. Jules mentions Largillière's *Portrait of a Lady as Pomona* twice. The painting he describes has exactly the same dimensions as the one on the German website:

> *Largillière Portrait of Vertumnus and Pomona*
> *The Regent and Madame de Parabère*
> *Considered Largillière's masterpiece*

This was exactly what Nadine had said! Though she'd apparently not realized it, she'd used precisely the same terms as Jules. She had forgotten nothing.

Farther down I read,

> *Collection Marquis de Chaponay*
> *Wildenstein*
> *Paraf*
> *Canvas in its magnificent original frame*
> *Reproduced in* Les Arts 1909
> *Largillière Exhibition at the Petit Palais, Paris*

There were a few words scribbled in pencil so faded I could barely decipher them. In 1928, Jules had made the purchase with the help of his son-in-law Roger Sorbac, whom he had repaid in 1935. Just beneath I managed to make out the words, "sold in 1941 for 400 MF." I guessed this meant 400 *milles francs,* 400,000 francs. I had no idea how much that sum would be equal to today.

I called Emmanuelle Polack to ask if she thought the picture might have been confiscated by the Nazis. The date of the sale, 1941, seemed significant. The first anti-Jewish laws had been decreed in October 1940, and the program of economic Aryanization was expanding, with many Jews selling their art because they needed ready cash in order to flee the country. The question I needed to answer was in what circumstances Jules had sold the Largillière.

Emmanuelle explained that we had to fill the gap in the painting's provenance, in other words to figure out through whose hands it had passed between 1938 and 1953.

It was not on the list of paintings Marie-Louise had put in a claim for after the war. Emmanuelle thought it was worth checking at the looted art archives in La Courneuve to see if it was on the list of confiscated artworks drawn up by Rose Valland and the French Commission for Art Recovery.

I always enjoyed going to La Courneuve with Emmanuelle. We joked about the glacial chill in the reading room, the endless waiting, the convoluted way the archives were classified, about everything and nothing. It was our way of fending off the gloomy atmosphere, the muted presence of persecuted families, whose letters, lists, and photos were shelved along the walls.

Emmanuelle pointed me toward the single computer terminal for consulting the digitized files of the Rose Valland archive. These were the index cards detailing the stolen works identified by the art recovery commission and noting whether or not they had been retrieved after the war. The looted artworks are classified by the name of the artist. As was my wont, I barely listened to her explanation and headed straight over to the computer terminal.

On the off chance, I typed in "Largillière." Incredibly, I immediately pulled up an index card filled in by someone on Rose Valland's team. It read,

Description: Madame de Parabère in a satin robe. Beside her, Prince Regent Philippe d'Orléans in an "extravagant bonnet (?)" whose mask, behind which he has been hiding, has just been removed by Love.

Name of owner: Jansson Cassagne Case, Intermediary for the Reichsbank account.

Address: 35 Avenue Charles Floquet and 42 Avenue Charles Floquet

Date of claim: 10th December 1945

Date of theft: Occupation

Circumstances of theft: Objects bought for the Reichsbank

See dossier Mungne Claim

Observations: sold

The dimensions were the same as those in Jules's notebook. There was no mention of him, but the painting appeared to be the same one. Why had it been stolen from a different address?

I took a photo of the screen and sent it to Henri. We spent the next few days trying to find out who Jansson Cassagne was, and what the "Mungne claim" referred to. But Google couldn't help us this time. Nor could the archives. The Jansson Cassagne Case remained a mystery.

A few weeks later I accompanied Emmanuelle to the Paris municipal archives, situated on the eastern edge of the city at Porte des Lilas. We entered the reading room like a couple of detectives sniffing out new clues. A curator was presenting to a group of German researchers a recently discovered archive of auctioneers' account ledgers, containing records of sales from 1940 to 1945. The detail sent a shiver down my spine. Emmanuelle gave me a discreet nod. I crept closer and took a few pictures.

These archives are not yet in the public domain. They are, however, invaluable for researchers and historians. Every auctioneer recorded the details of his sales at the Drouot auction house between 1940 and 1945. For example, in 1942 there was a sale with the title "Israelite Assets" that included plates, sewing machines, coffee jugs, and sheets. The Strausses were fortunate enough to have managed to hold on to essentials, but others had lost literally everything, including in some cases their means of making a living.

Every time I look at the pictures I took that day I feel an obscure sense of shame for being a treasure hunter on this ocean of "Jewish assets"; shame at the thought of the value of the Largillière, all the things I could buy myself with the money, even though I would be entitled to only a tiny percentage of its worth.

Emmanuelle wanted to show me some source material she was working on for her doctorate on the wartime art market. She had made some discoveries that would not please those in senior positions in French museums, and she risked making enemies of people in the very world in which she was hoping to make her career.

The sources she had found were called "Illicit Profits," dizzying lists (how many names, how many commissions?) of people who had been convicted of "doing business with the enemy," whatever their profession or business. Among them were art dealers, specialists, antique dealers, and auctioneers. There were also bakers, builders, cheesemakers, and tailors. They were tried after the war and the case files are now held in the Paris archives.

"Have you looked in Illicit Profits?" was a kind of password, a way of spotting an insider, a proper researcher. Gaining access to these files meant I was no longer considered a rank amateur.

Emmanuelle pointed me toward the alphabetically filed dossiers of those who were tried after the war. I found the name of André Schoeller, the dealer who in 1936 had bought, on behalf of a certain Monsieur Schwenck, Degas's *Portrait of*

Jacques de Nittis as a Child, one of the pictures on Andrew's original list, declared stolen by Marie-Louise. I took a photo.

When I showed it to Henri that evening, he murmured aloud the caption beneath it that I had somehow failed to notice: "Margot Jansson," then practically leapt out of his chair with excitement: "Jansson—as in the Jansson Cassagne Case, from the Valland index card!"

It was a discovery as improbable as it was miraculous: I'd stumbled upon a dossier on Margot Jansson. I had to wait a few days before being brought the folder of yellowing pages. The last traces of the story of a woman accused of dealing with the enemy. Perhaps I had finally found the key to the mystery of the Largillière.

Terrified as I was of tearing the paper, I was impatient to find out about the adventures of Margot Jansson, a Swedish-born woman who'd been working in Paris before the war as a salesgirl in an undergarments store. During the Occupation, she became an intermediary, brokering sales of works of art to the Nazis. I immersed myself in the details of her long-ago trial. There was a file detailing the accusation and a file detailing her defense. She was accused of procuring works of art on behalf of a certain Herr Doktor Wolff, of the Reichsbank, between 1941 and 1944, and of having taken large commissions. She was denounced by her secretary, Mademoiselle Nungné (not Mungne, as Rose Valland spelled it on the art recovery commission document).

In one of the Valland dossiers I found a copy of a catalog of the artworks that had been transported by Mademoiselle

Nungné, at the behest of her employer. A tantalizing list, with high prices to match, of around one hundred pieces of French Regency, Louis XIV and Louis XV-era furniture and tapestries. And one painting: *Portrait of a Lady as Pomona*: 4.5 million. Had the painting sold by Jules for 400,000 francs been sold on to the Reichsbank for 4.5 million, or was that merely the starting price?

Jules's painting seems to have passed through the hands of Margot Jansson, then sold to Herr Doktor Wolff, the architect of the Reichsbank. He wanted to decorate the bank like the Banque de France building in Paris, with eighteenth-century objects and paintings, all procured by Margot Jansson.

The chief inventory expert at the archives turned out to be an admirer of my brother Édouard's acting, so he invited me into his office and showed me the digitized Illicit Profits documents. He wanted to talk about my brother, while I wanted to know more about the postwar trials. Because he was a genuine fan of Édouard's humor, he offered to email me the documents. I liked the thought that my brother was helping me without knowing it, allowing me to save time and avoid spending hours hunched over lists that weren't even classified in alphabetical order.

This small underworld of art world intermediaries and scavengers had echoes of Patrick Modiano's novels. Would I ever find out the exact circumstances in which Jules had sold the Largillière? Had he handed it over directly to Madame Jansson? Was there another intermediary? Had he been forced to sell it for next to nothing? And if that were the case, how could I find out what it would have been worth in 1941? I wondered if it would be possible to compare it with another painting by Largillière sold in the same period. It was clear it had been a forced sale, but I needed hard evidence. Marie-Madeleine de Parabère had yet to give up all her secrets.

XXXIII

THE FORGOTTEN LETTER

In all my research, I'd forgotten the main protagonist, the picture itself.

In the Louvre documentation center, the index cards on each painting are classified according to era, artist, or theme. I searched both Largillière and "Portraits of well-known women," and here I came upon the meaning of its mythological theme. Marie-Madeleine de Parabère, the Regent's favorite, sitting with a pomegranate in her lap, is portrayed as the nymph Pomona, goddess of fruit trees and orchards. Behind her, the Regent is shown in the guise of Vertumnus, the god of the changing seasons. In Ovid's *Metamorphoses*, Vertumnus adopts multiple disguises to try to win Pomona's love. I wondered if Jules was particularly taken by the symbolism. Did he believe in eternal love? I was searching for a sign or a message, but perhaps there was none.

I found photocopies of documents about various exhibitions in which the painting was displayed. In a 1928 exhibition the painting was "lent by Roger Sorbac." By 1938 it was "from the Jules Strauss Collection." I knew that Jules had reimbursed Sorbac his share in 1935.

When I arrived that day, the dusty reading room was almost empty. I spotted the flushed face of the elderly retired curator, alternately pacing around his desk, muttering furiously, and busying himself with his boxes, apparently filing magazine articles and sheets of paper. I found a desk as far from him as possible. I was aware of him glaring at me, though I couldn't understand what it was about my presence that irritated him so much.

Slipped inside a catalog, I discovered a handwritten letter from 1973, written in poor French by a man named Harald Marx and addressed to a colleague at the Louvre, E. Macquart. Marx was a German art historian and had been curator of the Old Masters Picture Gallery in Dresden for almost forty years. He described the portrait of Madame de Parabère and listed its known provenance. Then he informed his colleague that it was in the Dresden museum and asked him,

> What do you know of the collection of the Marquis de Chaponay and what happened to this painting?
> We have a painting here like it. [. . .]. The portrait ended up in the gallery after the war, and we have been unable to establish its prewar provenance, that is, the portrait was sent here from the Nationalgalerie of Berlin with no documentation.

Astonishingly, the letter appeared to have remained unanswered. I carefully went through the contents of the box several times but found no reply to Herr Marx of Dresden.

It occurred to me that if anyone had bothered to respond, or tried to locate Jules Strauss or his descendants in 1973, the year I was born, I wouldn't have been in the archives that day, trying to flush out proof from these dusty old forgotten boxes.

I walked over to the desk of the reading room supervisor. She presided over the place with a regal air, though I wasn't entirely sure what her role was.

"Do you have any idea how I might contact Monsieur Macquart, the addressee of this letter?

"That's him, over there," she said, pointing to the elderly man.

"Oh! I thought he was retired."

"He is, but he still comes in every day."

Was he passionate about his job or an overly zealous civil servant who couldn't quite relinquish his job? If that was the case, surely he would be happy to help me.

I walked up to him with the letter from Dresden in my hand.

"Monsieur, I've found this letter, it's addressed to you, and I just wanted to ask you . . ."

He didn't let me finish.

"This is unbelievable!" He virtually spat at me, he was so angry.

He turned and marched out of the reading room, muttering heatedly to himself. I wasn't sure if he'd seen the letter I was holding. Was he simply furious at being bothered, or was it specifically the story of looted art that enraged him?

Something that hadn't occurred to me was now becoming clear. The cantankerous old man who had failed to respond to Harald Marx's letter was also, I now realized, the author of the article about Jules's donation of frames to the Louvre. Now he was refusing to speak to me. Did he hold some kind of grudge against my family? Against Jules, or Jewish collectors in general?

Baffled and frustrated, I went back to the reading room supervisor. She wasn't surprised. Yes, she agreed, he was rather odd.

"So you just leave him alone to do whatever he wants in the Louvre archives?" I asked her, puzzled. "Do you know what he's putting inside all those boxes?"

She shrugged her shoulders and smiled, as if to say, "What can I do about it?"

I left that evening with nothing more than a picture on my cellphone of an old letter from a Dresden museum curator. On my way home, I imagined the episode as a scene in a movie: a former curator returns to haunt the Louvre archives, destroying compromising documents and tearing up evidence against him, with me as the heroine, a modern-day Rose Valland, chasing him down corridors in hot pursuit, hoping to catch him in the act, and thus to save the archives of families whose art collections had been confiscated and whose pictures were languishing in the Louvre stacks.

XXXIV

A ROMANTIC WEEKEND IN DRESDEN

November 2017. Henri and I were spending the weekend in Dresden, in the former East Germany. We could have gone anywhere, but we'd chosen the city that had been almost completely destroyed in the Allied bombing and then rebuilt after the war. In the late autumn gloom, it didn't feel like a romantic weekend. On the program: four flights, a cheerless hotel, sausages for dinner, tossing and turning in bed, no sex, plenty of anxiety. The next day, three hours at the museum, failing to get permission to photograph the painting, and then the flight home, only too aware that this was just the beginning of our struggle for justice.

Henri warned me that the Germans were always ahead of the game. At midnight, he left the hotel to figure out the best way to get to the museum. I stayed behind in the hotel and ordered a cocktail in the brightly lit bar. I was trying to distract myself, to stop myself from obsessing over our case. I knew the details of the dossier like the back of my hand, but I was terrified I would lose my cool at our meeting, which I anticipated would be like a tribunal.

The next morning, we arrived at the Gemäldegalerie Alte

Meister, the Old Masters Picture Gallery, a little before the meeting was due to start. The three representatives from the museum were already there, seated behind a long table in the director's office. We were invited to take our seats across from them. A disconcertingly fat file sat on the table between us. I was so intimidated that I couldn't take in each person's job title. I must have come across as very solemn, as though all too aware of the gravity of the moment.

Seventy years after the fact, I had come to Dresden to represent my great-grandfather Jules Strauss, and demand the return of his painting, Largillière's *Portrait of a Lady as Pomona*.

It was immediately clear the museum's director, clearly the most Machiavellian of the three, was not keen to return the painting. His questions remain engraved in my memory:

"Perhaps Herr Strauss was happy to have sold his painting for a decent price?" he said, in heavily accented English.

The cynical remark reminded me of an early scene in Joseph Losey's 1976 film *Monsieur Klein*, in which Alain Delon plays an art dealer whose wartime business is buying up the possessions of Jews forced to flee. "It's easy enough to buy from someone who has no choice but to sell," one of his clients tells Klein.

"I am not obliged to buy from you," responds the dealer acerbically.

I reminded the museum director, calmly, of the anti-Jewish laws of October 1940, blocked bank accounts, Aryanized businesses.

Henri, too, kept emotion out of his voice as he reminded the director of certain key dates. It was facts that would rule in our favor, facts that saved us from sentimentality.

There followed three hours of tense, difficult discussion. No one raised their voice, of course. We had to justify our cause and furnish evidence that the painting belonged to the family and had been stolen by the Nazis. Henri and I had spent hours putting together the dossier, but we were unprepared for how upset we would be by the sense of injustice.

The painting had passed through the hands of Margot Jansson, who had procured dozens of paintings, tapestries, and pieces of furniture, including the Largillière, all destined to decorate the Reichsbank.

"But what proof do you have that Monsieur Strauss had not already sold it?"

We had to avoid using the term "forced sale." Let them reach that conclusion themselves. It was like a shadow boxing match, in which the opponents were no longer there.

"Yes, of course I'll send you everything I know about my great-grandfather. His notebooks, his life story, you'll have everything you need."

I was angry with myself for being so accommodating. When the meeting came to an end, I thanked them; it was not they who had robbed Jules, after all. But still I shook with silent fury. Was it mine, or that of Jules?

We were both upset. We spent the rest of the day at the museum. Unbelievably, we weren't even offered free entrance for our trouble. We wandered, aimlessly, our legs a little unsteady: we needed to look at beautiful things to temper the intensity of our emotions.

January 2018. Karolina Seidel, the Dresden museum's provenance researcher, had come to Paris to examine Jules's notebook, with the purpose of establishing definitively that the Largillière had belonged to him. We met at Elizabeth Royer's office on Place du Palais-Bourbon. Seidel wore white gloves to turn the pages, which she pored over for three hours. In the room next door, I paced up and down, unable to focus on anything else. What would she find that I had missed? What was she looking for exactly? She was polite without being warm, distant without being cold. I didn't know what to say to her. She was just doing her job, there was no emotion involved. I had no idea what she really thought or felt.

We would have to wait for her report, she told us before she left, then the museum director would get back to us. She didn't know when that would be.

XXXV

A FAMILY MEAL

"If anything happens to Nadine, you must let me know, I'll come over straightaway."

Michel and Sally were in Paris for a few days, and we met one day for lunch. Even though he was eighty, had spent several months in and out of hospital, and walked with some difficulty, it went without saying that he would cross the Channel for his cousin.

"Of course I'll call you."

I couldn't bear to even contemplate my aunt dying. She was my last connection with the Baer and Strauss families. I still had so many questions to ask her.

The day before we met, Michel rang to remind me to bring Jules's notebooks. I was hoping he would forget he'd lent them to me, they'd become my secret treasure that I moved from place to place around my bedroom. I'd never figured out where to store them, how to keep them safe, but I liked having them with me. They were companions during my research, as though they conjured Jules's presence. But they weren't mine; Marie-Louise had left them to Michel. I brought them to the restaurant, and kept them in their bag on my lap, hoping that Michel would forget to ask for them.

Andrew was late. He'd lost weight, and his hair had turned almost completely gray. He'd just got back from Brazil. It turned out that in August we'd both been in exactly the same area, in the northwest of the country. We'd taken the same photograph of the jetty at Tibau do Sul and gone on the same dune buggy excursion, just a few days apart. I don't know that I'd have been very pleased to bump into him on the beach.

Still, five years since we had first spoken about the subject that had come to obsess me, I was very happy to see my cousins again. I had the strange impression that we'd become very close, without really knowing each other or having any shared memories. I couldn't quite understand this strange connection, or my desire to please them both. Perhaps it was our shared affection for our forebears inciting me to make up for lost time.

There we were, the four of us, around a table in a fine restaurant, politely catching up with one another's news and chatting about our vacations. I asked Sally in English about her dogs, and Michel showed us photos of the Elizabethan portraits he'd recently acquired. I felt slightly ill at ease, my heart was thumping. It was obvious they'd organized this lunch for a specific reason, and their cool courteousness only added to my anxiety.

While we waited for our food to arrive, I recounted in minute detail my dealings with the Dresden museum, and the various ideas I had for trying to find other paintings. I shared, with naïve and no doubt tiresome enthusiasm, my various hunches and suspicions. In vain pursuit of praise and encouragement, I told them about the archives I'd been to and the historians I had met.

By the time our main course was served, Michel had still not explained the reason for our meeting. Could it have been simply for the pleasure of lunching with his family? After a good deal of digression, I finally worked out the purpose of our meeting: Michel and Andrew had discovered that the *Portrait of a Lady as Pomona* was worth a lot more money than they'd originally thought.

Eagerly, I told them I had written back to the museum and would follow up. I explained why we'd been waiting for so long. Michel gently put a stop to my babbling: what was needed, as he always said, was efficiency. He wondered if we should hire a lawyer—how about that French lawyer I kept bumping into at all those conferences on looted art? I thought we needed a German lawyer. The issue was how to know who to trust. I heard myself suggesting that I do some research into the matter. Once again, the zealous goody-two-shoes, taking notes, making lists. I'd have loved for them to help; they knew the art world inside out, they would have made much swifter progress, would have known whom to ask, which sources to consult. What had they been doing while I'd been making the rounds of the archives and flying to Dresden with Henri? But I didn't ask anything of them, merely took heed of their suggestions.

I was getting tired of the sound of my own voice and

the technical conversation. There was something I wanted to ask Michel.

"Do you feel Jewish?"

"I do, yes," he said.

"In what way?"

"How shall I put it . . . Whenever I meet people from abroad, and they tell me they're Jewish, we don't even need to say anything, there's a tacit bond between us," he said.

I formulated the question in a different way, as a way to get him to divulge something more personal.

"Well, when my father was dying, he made my mother promise not to bring me up Jewish," he said.

André died in 1939; was this last request linked to the rise of Nazism? Was André already aware of what was going to happen to the Jews, or was it simply that because he didn't feel Jewish himself, he didn't want his son to be? Why did it matter so much to him?

Michel was unaware of his grandfather's request that his ashes be scattered in a common grave. In fact, Jules was buried in the Père-Lachaise cemetery, between Marie-Louise and André. Michel said he would like to be buried there, too, but there was no room. He didn't want to be cremated or buried near his house in England, with Sally, or in Oxford, where his mother was buried, but with his father in Paris, where he had never lived. He wanted to be buried with the Strausses.

Andrew suggested we go to visit his grave together. I didn't tell him I'd been just a few days earlier, and had got completely lost looking for the family vault in the Jewish section, among the monuments honoring those who had died in the concentration camps. Map in hand, I wandered for two hours in the rain. I twisted my ankle on the cobbles of the long circular paths that kept leading me back to where I'd started. I peered at gravestones and tried to keep away from the crowds of tourists who had come to see the graves of Édith Piaf, Oscar Wilde, and Jim Morrison. And I found nothing, no monument or stone façade carved with the name Strauss. I emptied my little pot of flowers at the entrance and took it home with me on the metro.

As our meal came to an end, Michel announced, quite out of the blue and with an impish expression:

"I am the heir to Jules Strauss. I embody the 'Strauss sensibility.'"

There was certainly one thing we all had in common, the family trait of jumping from one subject to another. (Nadine was the expert.) I couldn't help but be moved by this old man proclaiming himself the descendant of a man whom he'd barely known.

And yet even as I thought this, I felt an absurd little burst of jealousy: What made him the heir of our venerated forebear, just because he'd had a career in the art world, because he had an "eye"? Wasn't I also Jules's heir? I might not have any artistic sensibility, but something else linked us, even if I couldn't put a name to it. I liked to think that there was a certain complicity between Jules and me.

We stood up to leave, and embraced one another warmly.

I had, alas, to give Michel back Jules's notebooks. I was exhausted. Having hoped they would offer me their help, that we'd work together, all that had happened was I'd ended up promising to do even more.

I watched Michel and Sally walk away down the street. He was limping. I hoped he was on the road to recovery.

That evening, my son, Élie, asked me how much money I'd get if we recovered the Largillière. Would I get more than the others since I was the one who'd done all the work?

"I'm not in this for the money, you know," I told him.

"But without you, they'd never even have found the painting! How much do you think you'll get when it's sold?"

Élie was seventeen, and beginning to think about his future, about his job prospects, how much he might earn. He was already imagining the apartment he was going to buy before he was thirty. He couldn't understand why I was working for nothing. He sighed, deeply disappointed that his mother was apparently incapable of asserting her rights. He even drafted a letter on my behalf asking the rest of the family that I be remunerated for the all the work I'd done. I didn't send it.

What kind of an example was I setting Élie, if I couldn't even confess to what I truly wanted? How could I admit to my son I was a bit of a coward when it came to asking for money? I wasn't being very honest with myself either, because deep down I knew that money was not what I was after. Even more than my family's recognition and gratitude, I wanted to tell him, what I truly yearned for was to be able to say that I had, at last, achieved something with my life.

XXXVI
A VERY LONG WAIT

I wrote, a letter, in my best English, to the director of the Dresden museum:

> *Dear Dr. Pr. Müller and Ms. Seidel,*
>
> *I would like to know where you stand with regard to the restitution of the Largillière painting, Portrait de Madame de Parabère.*
>
> *After our meeting in Dresden in November 2017, Ms. Seidel's visit in Paris to look at Jules Strauss's notebooks in February, Dr. Pr. Müller's e-mail in March, we are keen to know whether your diligence is done and what is the process going forward.*
>
> *Jules Strauss's heirs are getting old, his 4 grandsons are now between 80 and 97-year-old. And three of them do not have much time left.*
>
> *They would like Jules Strauss's painting back in their family before they die.*
>
> *Please let me know what you are willing to do.*

It was now almost eighty years after the paintings had

been expropriated, and over seventy-five years since Marie-Louise Strauss had put in her claim for the return of the stolen works of art. I'd spent the previous two years tracing the confusing journey of the *Portrait of a Lady as Pomona* from Paris to Dresden, via Berlin and the vaults of the Reichsbank.

How had my great-grandfather's painting ended up on display in Dresden for over twenty years, without anyone ever really trying to find out whom it belonged to?

Place de la Madeleine, November 2018. We finished off the last crumbs of our sandwiches in Henri's office, minutes before a decisive phone meeting with the Dresden museum. We went through what we were going to say one more time. What was the restitution process? How would the final decision be made, and by whom? What were the next stages?

We put the call on speakerphone to talk with Professor Müller, the museum's head of research, and Karolina Seidel, the provenance researcher whom I had met in Paris. Müller was organizing a major conference for the twentieth anniversary of the Washington Principles on Nazi–Confiscated Art.

"We would like to keep the painting," he said by way of introduction, in his heavily accented English. "We have come to the conclusion that there was indeed a forced sale, but the circumstances were complicated. Therefore, we would like to buy the painting from you."

I was completely flummoxed. One year since we had first met, two years after we'd begun negotiations, now they were telling us they wanted the painting to remain in the museum. I didn't know what to say. I let Henri speak.

"How do you suggest we proceed?" he asked.

"We would like to meet with the Strauss family to agree on a price. The painting will be returned to you, and then you will sell it to us."

Is a restitution with conditions attached really a restitution?

"What happens if we fail to come to an agreement?" Henri asked.

Müller explained that the museum would deliver its conclusions about the forced sale to the federal Ministry of Art and Culture, the body that would make the final decision. There was a possibility that the restitution would be refused.

I was absolutely furious, but I didn't know how to respond. Henri told the director that we would discuss it with the rest of the family and decide what to do. We asked if we could read their dossier and their conclusions about the Largillière. The conversation ended on a polite note. But their offer disgusted me, and I ranted to Henri for several minutes after the call. This was a second forced sale! A restitution that was conditional on us agreeing to sell the painting to the museum. It wasn't about the money. The money they gave us would never be enough. Why not, Henri asked. It was true that if we sold them the Largillière afterward, it would end up being sort of the same thing.

No. Restitution is a way of acknowledging persecution. When they spoke of "complicated" circumstances, and forced us to agree to sell back the painting, was this not, in a way, denying that it had been stolen—and thus negating Jules's history?

I needed to find the final, irrefutable proof that the painting had been expropriated. I had a strong sense that I would find something; if only I could put my hands on evidence that Jules's bank account had been blocked, or that he had been forced to pay the tax imposed on the Jews.

If I couldn't find anything, would I be obliged to accept the museum's conditions?

The portrait didn't belong in Germany. I didn't know if I had the courage and the patience to keep fighting for it. But I did know that I wanted to keep the portrait, hang it on the wall in my living room, live with Madame de Parabère, all five feet of her, with her serene smile and inscrutable expression. I didn't want to sell it, either to a museum or an individual. I wanted her to talk to me, to tell me about Jules, about how she'd been passed from one owner to another, how she had gone through the war, over borders, across time.

January 2019. One cold and rainy morning, after dropping my daughters at school, I spotted Patrick Modiano in the distance. Though I was sure he had no desire to be recognized or bothered at this time of the morning, I ran to catch up with him. We resumed the conversation we had begun two years earlier:

"I spoke to the director of the Dresden museum on the phone; he said they'd only return the painting if we agreed to sell it right back to them," I told him.

"How funny, I have cousins in Dresden," he replied. I liked the way his words always headed off in some unexpected direction. The end of every sentence was always a surprise.

He smiled, expressed concern, was so quick-witted and sensitive that even the briefest conversation seemed to encompass so much more than just the two of us.

I didn't need to explain to him why I wanted to see the painting again, why I wanted to bring it back from Germany. I knew he was thinking the same. Even if I were never to see Madame de Parabère again, I felt less alone just knowing this.

We said goodbye. I watched him as he continued along the street toward his wife, who smiled warmly at me from a distance as she took him affectionately by the arm.

I went on my way to meet some mothers from school at a café, but as we sat drinking coffee on the terrace, chatting about children and vacations, I was thinking how I'd like to run and catch up with the Modianos, walk across the Luxembourg Gardens with them, without talking. I wanted our thoughts to fly up on a smile to some other sky, some other moment in time.

I imagined Modiano as a child, my daughters' age, running along the park's gravel paths, down rue Bonaparte all the way to Place Saint-Sulpice, skipping along the banks of the Seine to the family apartment on the Quai de Conti. A little farther on is the apartment my newly married father moved into a few years later, on the quay opposite the Louvre, mere steps away from the antique dealers with whom he remained on first name terms until the end of his life, and whose establishments he continued to frequent even after he grew so frail that I would follow him at a discreet distance, worried he might fall. I still live in that same part of town. Every day I walk past galleries whose former owners might have been among those who bought up the art of persecuted Jews during the Occupation.

I thought of Jules, strolling along the Quai Voltaire, peering into gallery windows in search of rare treasures, and of my grandmother Nicole, who sold folk art in a shop called *Le Distrait* a few streets away. I remembered being a little girl, racing home from school and clambering onto her lap to sing old French *chansons* that in turn I sang to Élie, and that my daughters, Rose and Colombe, still love today.

EPILOGUE

THE PAINTING'S LONG JOURNEY HOME

September 2019. The *Portrait of a Lady as Pomona* was still hanging in the museum in Dresden.

At last, after four years of research and requests for the painting to be returned to the family, the museum director sent me a message: "Really good news! A few minutes ago I received the message that our Ministry of Finance finally agreed!" I called Nadine to give her the good news.

"Well, I will no longer be around," she replied. She could barely walk any more, but she was still completely on the ball. I protested, "Of course you will. This is really it this time!"

But it turned out I'd cried victory a little prematurely. When, a few months later, I read through the four pages of the "Protocol for the Restitution of the *Portrait of a Lady as Pomona* to the Descendants of Jules Strauss" sent by the museum, I discovered that it wasn't justice after all. The German curators acknowledged neither the theft of the painting nor the conditions of the forced sale. The repetition of the phrase "it is not impossible that" didn't seem to be merely a problem of translation. I was unable to sign.

Although the German Museum Association had officially declared its willingness to atone for crimes of the past by returning expropriated works of art to their owners, the law was vague, and for two years our request for the return of the Largillière had been passed around between the museum, the Ministry of Arts and Culture, and the Finance Ministry.

Since it was a political decision, we needed a means to put pressure on the relevant bodies. One evening, at the end of a fundraising dinner for the Shoah Memorial in Paris, I rushed up to the man my neighbor at dinner had pointed out as the German ambassador to France; he heard me out, then said, "You need to speak to the ambassador." I'd got it wrong—the actual ambassador was already halfway down the stairs. I caught up with him and, speaking in a rush, tried to engage him in conversation:

"Mr. Ambassador, my family has been waiting two years for a painting to be returned to us from the Dresden art museum. We've given them all the evidence they've asked for, but the museum is still refusing to return it."

He handed me his card.

Henri discovered an engraving of Madame de Parabère on a website, which he bought and had framed in accordance with Jules's taste. It's really thanks to him that I didn't give up. Whenever I lost heart, he would take over, writing letters to the museum with additional information. A friend of his, who knew the French ambassador in Berlin, agreed to help us. I couldn't get over it. He taught me the meaning of perseverance.

One day, in a café near my daughters' school, a father I barely knew told me how his relatives had escaped the Warsaw ghetto and fled to New York during the war. My childhood friend Sophie, who became strictly Orthodox after her marriage, told me about a great-uncle who had been deported, whose name was never mentioned at home. My old friend Franck was keenly following my research and hoping I might be able to help him find some trace of his grandmother, an artist whose paintings had simply vanished. I wrote down names of galleries and dates of exhibitions and pinned them on the wall above my desk. An elderly gentleman solicited my help; he seemed a bit confused but remembered with absolute clarity all the details—addresses, dates, and times— of the arrests of the members of his family. He wanted to locate the stamp collection built up by his Romanian-born great-uncle, a famous magician before the war. Back in the Police Archives, I went through files dealing with the arrest of immigrant Jews.

I could have set up an agency for people researching their family histories.

In September 2019 an exhibition called "Degas at the Opéra" opened at the Musée d'Orsay. I went the day it opened. I hadn't seen the catalog, but I had a sixth sense that one of Jules's pictures would be included in the show. I strode through the galleries, turned a corner, and found myself face-to-face with it: a painting of a group of dancers I had first seen in Edinburgh. The painting had a strange, greenish tint, not dissimilar to the color of the coat I was wearing. Degas had painted it toward the end of his life, when he was almost blind, and it's a little blurred, almost tentative even. The single line in the catalog and on the wall panel detailing the painting's provenance noted that it had been purchased by Jules Strauss in 1922. I wrote to the exhibition curator, who knew no more than I. What had happened to the painting between 1922 and 1952, when it was bought by the London gallery Arthur Tooth & Sons? For several months, Michel, Andrew, and I tried to piece together the painting's genealogy, to fill the mysterious gap in its provenance, without success. But I wasn't prepared to give up until I knew its entire history.

Long after Jules's collection had vanished, the pictures had continued their journey. That summer, when I was a guest at the country house belonging to my friend Agathe David-Weill's family, I saw on the wall of her father's bedroom, to the left of the bed, a nude by Delacroix, *Mademoiselle Rose*. I recognized it from the 1920 photograph of Jules's study.

Agathe was horrified. "Was it stolen?"

"No, no, after Jules sold it in 1932 it passed through the hands of several collectors. It crossed continents. Then one day your father bought it."

I was pleased to see it there. Paintings travel, they bear witness to our lives, our reversals of fortune. This one had found its way from Jules's study between the wars to the bedroom of an elderly banker who still enjoyed *Mademoiselle Rose*'s company. My daughter Rose is Agathe's goddaughter; *Mademoiselle Rose* clearly had a cheeky sense of humor and an impeccable sense of timing.

When I was twenty, I went to England to study for a year. That was when I first discovered the job of travel writer. Then and there I decided, without having any idea of what it involved, that I had found my vocation.

The mantelpiece in my bedroom is where I keep the souvenirs of this journey, pictures of my extended family: a melancholy portrait of Jules, another of him looking debonair alongside Marie-Louise, my father posing in his tank during the war, the photo of the Baer and Sorbac cousins as children, playing on a beach in Brittany. Alongside these family portraits is a postcard of the *Portrait of Jacques de Nittis as a Child*, about which someone once wrote: "This child could not have been painted without love."

I kept Michel and Andrew abreast of the slow progress of the restitution of the Largillière painting. I wasn't sure if it was time or perspective, but I felt very close to them both. I felt particularly grateful to Andrew for having set me on this strange path and allowing me to feel my way on my own. Jacques had died since the ceremony to return the Tiepolo, and Nadine was now ninety-five. There was no time to lose.

In January 2021, a few months after this book was published in France, in the midst of the Covid pandemic, the Staatliche Kunstsammlungen Dresden, which controls the holdings of the Old Masters Picture Gallery, finally returned the *Portrait of a Lady as Pomona* to its rightful owners.

The museum authority decided to accede, thanks to the solid dossier of documentation I had compiled with the assistance of a brilliant lawyer specializing in art restitution cases, along with support from the French Embassy in Germany and that of Germany in France. I wondered if the museum now genuinely wished to return the painting or if it was just giving into political pressure.

And so on a brisk, sunny morning, a German truck drove into the courtyard of my Parisian apartment building, from which two men who spoke only German pulled out a large, well-wrapped wooden crate. Madame de Parabère was too big for the elevator. She had to be carried up the stairs. I fussed nervously around the painting, terrified that something might happen to the Lady of Pomona. I felt a little weepy at this extraordinary situation, aware that her departure from France eighty years earlier, in plain sight of Jules and Marie-Louise, would have been strangely similar.

In the sitting room, the two moving men carefully unwrapped the painting and hung it on the wall using hooks known as *griffes du Louvre,* the most solid and secure. Every maneuver made me tremble. At last the men left, leaving behind some documentation from the Dresden museum that I barely glanced at.

Without taking off the masks we wore because of the Covid pandemic, Henri and I stood in silence for several minutes in front of the painting. We'd kept the promise we'd made to her three years earlier in the Dresden storerooms. After a long journey, Madame de Parabère was back in her home country.

Our joyful reunion was tinged with a slight apprehension. It felt like a huge responsibility. Was it really reasonable to want to keep in our apartment a painting that belonged to the whole family, that had traversed history and national borders? Wasn't it too valuable, too big, too fragile?

Friends and family came over to admire it. Everyone offered an opinion, noticed some detail, admired the power of her presence, paused to marvel at the directness of her gaze, her coiffure, her draped dress, the harmony of the colors. Visitors waxed lyrical about the split pomegranate she was holding, then peered a little more closely at the other fruits, rendered with such realistic detail. People telephoned and sent articles about Marie-Madeleine de Parabère and Philippe d'Orléans.

Could we keep her, or would we have to sell her? What is she worth, what condition is she in? I have no idea, but now, whenever we are alone and sitting on the couch facing the painting, we feel blessed. Occasionally we feel nostalgic. Our adventure is over, but we relish every second of our reunion.

Sometimes I walk past without seeing her. Other times, when the house is empty, the children at school, the cat purring on the couch, I pause in front of the portrait. We look knowingly at each other. Only I understand the journey she has taken, only she understands my quest.

I look at her and smile. More than a sense of victory, I feel calm, serene. No more uncertainty or anxiety. Everything is alright.

I don't go to the archives that often anymore, but recently I returned, a little nostalgically, to the Paris Archives on Boulevard Sérurier, where a couple of years into my investigation I had finally found, after months and months of searching, the requisition order for the Strauss apartment at 60 Avenue Foch. I'd started looking for it after my conversation with Patrick Modiano. I knew there was a volume listing the addresses of high-ranking Nazis and organizations, but it had been mislaid, and the head archivist took months to find it.

When an entire building was expropriated, the French police would draw up a precise description of the site, including its communal areas, with details of each apartment. For 60 Avenue Foch, there was a full page with a table listing the names of the tenants on each floor, from the first to the fifth, with the date of requisition, number of rooms, surface area, number of chimneys, blocked up or not. *Salvago, de Rivaud, Munoz, vacant, Propper, Leoboldi, de Estrada, Toulouse-Lautrec, Goukassow, Tinardon, Gonsalez, vacant, Strauss.* From these vertical columns and horizontal rows materialized an entire building, as though in cross section: so many forgotten lives and long-dead neighbors.

As I read, I was transported back in time to Jules and Marie-Louise's apartment. I saw two children, my father and

Nadine, playing among the art in the grand entrance hall. Jules, in his study, drawing up a list in his notebook of the paintings and objects to be put in storage for safekeeping. I pictured Kurt Maulaz throwing fancy parties in the drawing room. And Marie-Louise, returning alone after the war to an apartment echoing with memories.

But I stopped turning the brittle pages, afraid they would crumble into dust. I slipped the documents back into their sleeve, wrapped it in the thick, soft sheet of kraft paper that served as a folder, and tied it up with string. With a heavy heart, I took it up to the archivist's desk, and asked, "Please, do you think you could you find a box to protect this? This is my family."

ACKNOWLEDGMENTS

I have received so much help throughout my research, not only from friends and family, but also from the many strangers with whom I have shared this story. I would like to thank each and every one for their kindness, whatever form it took; to express my gratitude for their unstinting empathy and support; and to acknowledge the generosity with which everyone has responded to my questions, offered me advice and shared valuable information, without which my quest would have come to nothing.

First, I must thank my husband, Henri, who has accompanied me every step of the way with steadfast help, support, and advice, during both the research and the writing of this book. He has always had more faith in me than I do in myself.

Nadine, my beloved aunt, repository of our family's memory, without whom I wouldn't have known where to begin, who has patiently answered my endless questions.

Andrew Strauss, who trusted me and set me on the track of our family history.

Michel Strauss, who generously shared his memories, documents, and knowledge.

My brothers' creativity and talent inspire me every day. Thank you, Julien, without whose daily advice and encouragement I would never have been able to finish this book. And Édouard, upon whom I know I can always depend.

To my beloved and generous mother, Isabelle Baer, who knows so many things and from whom I still have so much to learn.

What joy it has been to discuss our family with my cousins Marie-Laure and Marie-Hélène Sorbac. To you, Marie-Hélène, I owe thanks for listening, supporting, and helping. Your father, the war hero Jacques Sorbac, a brave and unassuming man, is always in my thoughts.

Thank you, Claude Sorbac, for answering my questions. Apologies for not having come to see you.

Emmanuelle Polack, a brilliant art historian and provenance researcher, who taught me everything. My gratitude and admiration are boundless.

Elizabeth Royer, looted art provenance researcher, without whose generosity and drive all my attempts to find out what had happened would have been in vain.

Alexis Kugel, my affable, knowledgeable, and ever-present mentor.

Agathe David-Weill, my lifelong friend, who believed in my project, and her father, Michel David-Weill.

Denis Gombert, devoted friend, always patient and judicious with his advice.

Colombe Schneck, for encouraging me in my dream of writing a book.

Virginie Bloch-Lainé, for her generous friendship.

Stéphane Foenkinos, whose opinion is so important to me.

Laetitia and Timothée de Fombelle, each of whom in their own way encouraged me to tell this story.

Dominique Modiano, whose enthusiasm and generosity sustained me all through my research and writing.

Patrick Modiano, without whose prodigious memory I would never have learned my family's story, and whose novels have been my guide throughout.

Iman Bassalah, the best life coach one could wish for, who has followed every stage of the writing of this book, advising and encouraging me with benevolence and patience.

My publishers, Manuel Carcassonne, Alice d'Andigné, and Léa Marty, for their eagle-eyed attention and encouragement.

I would also like to thank the publishers who read my work in progress:

Dorothée Cuneo, for her enthusiasm, perceptiveness, and generosity.

Thomas Simonnet, for his close reading and enlightening suggestions.

Guillaume Robert and Antoine Caro, for their faith in me.

All my gratitude to Audrey Azoulay, thanks to whom Tiepolo's *Shepherd* was returned to the family.

David Zivie who, at every stage of his mission at the Ministry of Culture, gave freely and generously of his help.

Claudia Ferrazzi, who always swung immediately into action.

Her Excellency Ambassador Anne-Marie Descôtes.

Julien Acquatella, of the Berlin archive of the CIVS (Commission for the Compensation of Victims of Spoliation).

His Excellency Ambassador Nikolaus Meyer-Landrut.

And to the many experts, archivists, provenance researchers, and historians, without whose generosity I would never have been able to undertake this research, my gratitude for guiding me through their archives.

Marc Masurovsky, the exceptionally knowledgeable historian and author of *The ERR Project*, has done extensive research on the Strauss family, which he shared with me in thrilling emails.

Helena Patsiamanis, librarian in the conservation department of the Musée d'Orsay, gave me invaluable help in researching provenance.

Sébastien Chauffour, head of the art restitution archives at the INHA (National Institute of Art History), for his unwavering support.

Vincent Tuchais, archivist at the Paris Archives, for his help with my research and for guiding me through the archives.

Thomas Weber, expert on Hitler and a dear friend from our time together at Oxford, who introduced me to two people in particular who made my research possible:

Carolin Lange, whose research proved decisive, and Marius Mazziotti, who was an invaluable guide through various German archives.

Anne Heilbronn, who advised me early on, with her great sense of friendship.

Jean-Marc Dreyfus, who offered me generous assistance during my research.

Laurence Bertrand Dorléac, whose own fight for justice and unbending moral rectitude paved the way.

Doreen Carvajal, Bernadette Murphy, and Be⌒
of the Orphan Art Project, for their commitment in support
of spoliated families.

Corinne Hershkovitch, for her multiple fights on behalf
of those seeking justice.

David Foenkinos, François-Louis a'Weng, Sylvine
Bailly, Isabelle Bakouche, Franck Bussi, Galerie Chevalier,
M. and Mme Gérard Durand, Flavie Durand-Ruel, Monica
Dugot, Guillaume Gallienne, Adriana Gonzalez Hassig,
Simon Goodman, Cyril Grange, Stanka Jeleva, Patricia
Kennedy Grimsted and the team from the ERR Project,
Thomas Hervé, Sevan Matossian, Marianne Le Morvan,
Marc Liztler, Agnès Marconnet, Bertrand Meaudre, Anne
de Lacretelle, Nadia Lakhdar, Aline Le Visage, Lorraine
de Meaux, Alain Monteagle, François Nemer, Nathalie
Neumann, Youlia Nikolova, Emmanuel and Nathalie Patron,
Julia Pavlowitch, Agnès Peresztegi, Anne Roquebert, Jean
Rousselot, Philippe Rudaz, Paul Salmona, Achim Spelten,
Anne-Laure Sol, Philippe Sprang, Claire Touchard, Juliette
Trey, Clémence de Weck.

WORKS CITED

p. 50   Michel Strauss, *Pictures, Passions and Eye: A life at Sotheby's*, London, Halban, 2011.

p. 59   Corinne Bouchoux, *Si les tableaux pouvaient parler . . .* , *Le traitement politique et médiatique des retours d'œuvres d'art pillées et spoliées par les nazis, (1945–2008)*, Rennes, Presses universitaires de Rennes, 2013.

p. 59   Laurence Bertrand-Dorléac, *L'art de la défaite (1940–1944)*, Paris, Seuil 2010.

p. 59   Michel Rayssac, *L'exode des musées. Histoire des œuvres d'art sous l'Occupation*, Paris, Payot, 2007.

p. 103 André de Fouquières, *Mon Paris et ses parisiens, le quartier de l'Étoile*, Paris, Pierre Horay, 1953.

p. 118 Emmanuelle Polack, *Le marché de l'art sous l'Occupation, 1940–1944*, Paris, Tallandier, 2019.

p. 129 Patrick Modiano, *Discours à l'Académie suédoise*, Paris, Gallimard, 2015.

p. 133 Patrick Modiano, *Un pedigree*, Paris, Gallimard, 2005.

p. 182 Olivier Guez, *La disparition de Joseph Mengele*, Paris, Grasset, 2017.

p. 183 Alice Zeniter, *L'art de perdre*, Paris, Flammarion, 2017.

p. 183 Patrick Modiano, *Dora Bruder*, Paris, Gallimard, 1997.

PAULINE BAER DE PERIGNON is a journalist and screenwriter. Based in Paris, she has been a literary director in the audiovisual sector for over ten years, and regularly runs writing workshops as part of the 'Atelier de Pauline'. *The Vanished Collection* is her first book.

NATASHA LEHRER is a writer, translator and editor. Her journalism has appeared in publications including the *Guardian*, *Observer* and *TLS*, and she has translated books by Georges Bataille, Chantal Thomas and the Dalai Lama. Her co-translation of Nathalie Léger's *Suite for Barbara Loden* won the 2017 Scott Moncrieff Prize.